24
Sequential
Philosophic
Essays

(Sept. 1995 – Mar. 1996)

★

Traumear

Paperback ISBN 978-0-244-73306-3

*

www.traumear.com

Index of titles

*

These essays, except for two exceptions, were written to the format of exactly ten manuscript pages.

They enlarge on various concepts that occurred spontaneously to the author during the course of the writing, so they do not adhere to a preconceived plan. They will be appreciated by those who like to contemplate some of the finer points of the practical human spirit's achievements. As mature human beings we are able to do much for our fellow humans by learning the power of compassion and using it to solve life problems for those not quite as advanced as ourselves. The great challenge for our century is the evolution- or resurrection-growth of those who are called or even chosen to evolve to the point of completion, however they have little or no understanding of what is involved. As a consequence they mistake the often painful challenges to their creative capacities for avoidable misfortunes and grief rather than perceiving them as means towards communal reality and eternal life.

One of the tasks of such essays is to update modern vocabulary for the expression of reality from the contemporary point of view; this, by and large, is contextually managed.

*

1

Philosopher

A philosopher has to keep in training or people will run him ragged. He begins to eat and drink, and he looks for his comforts. Then comes the shock. It should be a guarantee for him, when it comes. He has not been forsaken, in spite of his laziness.

He may argue he has only given his mind a holiday. But philosophy wants the whole man, not just the mind. The entire human being is the instrument on which philosophy disports itself, so whatever part of himself the man has neglected to add into the equation bites him from behind now and he wonders, momentarily, how he has deserved it.

But that only wastes time, that wondering. The philosopher never asks for very long, only for the time of a blind reaction: "What have I done wrong?" He asks instead, as soon as possible after the shock has worn off: "How can I put this experience to good use?" because it makes no sense to him that mistakes should not have been made. Who can judge? He is also, among other things, a child of his time and shares in his compatriots' tendencies and liabilities. Would he rather be a robot, and not vulnerable? Then let him run a newspaper, or manage an airline company, or something for which he can be one hundred and ten percent insured in case of error.

A lucky find – is what a true philosopher calls his mistakes. He may have wandered too far into the realm of spirit. Very well, he finds that out as soon as he pays the penalty. But he also pays for a new discovery, for a new angle on an old conviction. If all he could see was the penalty, why then that in itself would be the next mistake, and so on, until he came to himself and to the heroic point of view. He was born to that point of view, and if he strays from it he finds no rest.

Rest, for the philosopher, is a vital statistic. Without rest, either as an ambition or a memory, or perhaps even as a sensation, he cannot live. And yet he would definitely live. Death is a shameful existence for him. If his life runs out he begins to accuse himself, to abuse himself too. He scratches his soul until it bleeds. Next time – so he promises himself while in the throes of death – he will certainly invest in rest, come hell or high water.

Even that resolution suffices. All becomes still around him. The world is as it was prior to the initial creative contact. What he experiences is not rest but a foreshadowing of it. That will have to do him for the moment. This stillness of the world, with him alert at the centre like a nervous predator, gives him an indication of the sort of thing he is after. He has it outside him at the moment. He wants it within him – and everywhere, eventually. So now he gets to work.

Never imagine that the beginning is pleasant for him. Let's face it, he has to distance himself from an experience people around him would 'clutch' if they had it. Which is, of course, why they never have it – unless their time is up. One way to doom an individual is to expose him to this image of rest. He will never live it down. It eats him up. Cases like this are reported in the newspapers.

So the work begins with the rejection of this state of apparent rest. If the philosopher has an artistic bent he will have to overcome that or the result will be gloom and doom and morbidity. He must dig keeper, into himself, into the totally unknown, into regions where the external lassitude and relaxation cannot reach. The pleasant, convenient self-satisfaction gets the rug pulled out from under it. Immediately demons attack. They smell fresh soul and they want their share. The philosopher has any number of contemporary scandals to contend with now. He has been in touch with his contemporaries, he has rubbed up against them and he shares in the collective opprobrium. The common enemy of the race is about to choose him as his battlefield. The resulting pressures threaten to be immense. The moon-lit scene has yielded to pandemonium.

How can the man who has taken this step of assigning the falsehood its rightful name and place now contain himself? Why is he not overrun? Whence his strength in the face of multitudinous accusation? Unleashed in his soul – the wrath of disturbed complacency. Any part of himself the philosopher cannot rely on now. His spirit turns this way and that way, looking for direction which is not forthcoming. His flesh lies under a ban, paralyzed from the waist down and petrified from the crotch up. His mind is as vacant as a disused airstrip; he could not think if he tried, and he knows better than to try. His body, let's face this too, is nonexistent. Vision, if activated, would serve the enemy. The enemy is prowling outside the gates. Not a feeling or emotion, not a passion may be risked. His body is a clean slate. And his soul as such, well, he must take it for granted; he certainly has no evidence of it. If he did, it would be false evidence, later to be held against him.

What is left, with all these faculties out of action? Let's not rush into an answer to this question. The philosopher, as he works away here, may go over his ground again and again until he is quite sure of one thing, namely, that nothing about him could appeal to his enemy, the false one, the pretender. He is willing to hold out even longer than necessary, longer than polite; until finally he knows that he stands there with absolutely nothing to show for himself or to plead for himself than – himself. Mind you, he knows who he is. This fact alone makes him worthy to do battle for the race. He knows who he is, though nothing adheres to him that would allow anyone else to point to him and say: "That one is like me!" He has stepped outside the likeness-relation with others and he has offered himself for the truth-relation with them. The task required optimum thoroughness and then some. Rigorous abstraction in terms of memory, imagination and fantasy has removed him beyond the pale for the crowd of maligners and well-wishers alike. They cannot any longer recognize him, the flatterers and the critics, so they give up on him. A few compliments, a few missiles are thrown, but they bounce back into the face of those who threw them. The lesson is soon learned: This one is off-limits; this one is taboo.

The man who stops here, safe within limits, off-side in a sense peculiar to the public and to himself, is not a philosopher but a crank. Such cranks abound in the world and their confessions of crankiness are often reckoned in their favour, because they manage to stay put somewhere, in an environment where others either fade or explode. The crank demonstrates his inviolability by inventing a multitude of artificial little enemies for himself which cannot, of course, hurt him. His 'works', if they must be called something, are responses to self-flagellation. The hermit, the monk – these laboratory technicians which have their representatives and emulators in every age, even today – or perhaps especially today, when time, space and causality are tricked out of existence (nearly) by so many – what shall we call them – super-people. They never exist in the singular but attached to some famous or notorious specialty which ends by surrounding them like an aura.

When the true philosopher, not one of the super-people, stands exposed, he does not quickly rush to boast about his achievement of abstraction as if the aim of it had been to demonstrate his power, but he waits and sees. This generic waiting and seeing is not very glamorous, but for that reason all the more effective – towards something which the philosopher only dimly intuits; he cannot put his finger on it. Plenty of opportunities arise for putting his finger on things; he rejects them all. He may take a short walk through the world, open-eyed and – anonymous. A stroll into a supermarket suits him. He may even make a small purchase, because one does that sort of thing in supermarkets, not because he needs anything. What interests him above all for the time being is anonymity. If he must be addressed, let it be under a false name. Usually he has no money at this stage, but that is no precondition, only a matter of personal predilection.

Let it be said in all honesty: he may wait for years. He may wait even beyond his removal from earth. When asked: "How long?" he answers: "As long as it takes." One wonders what he means. What, precisely, is the philosopher's reward?

For years, maybe, he waits and sees; not like the crank, who right away goes in for self-advertising, under one respectable name or another, but like a hawk on a thermal current, or like a wildcat behind a bit of brush near a waterhole. His waiting and seeing is the second stage, or period, of his work. The first period comprised his abstraction from himself of all that was not himself, and, depending on his upbringing, or on his lack of upbringing, and also of course on his individual temperament, this may have amounted to a fair lot. Finally he stood revealed, not to the world but to reality. His works of abstraction have accumulated. Those who desire to find out who they are, or more likely those who may care to discover whether or not they are, can make good use of these works. He did them equally for himself and for them. Then, perhaps after a short flirtation with crankiness, to wear down his teeth a little and to sharpen his claws, he proceeds to the period of work which allows him to assert his individuality and to keep it in trim. He makes very few excursions into the realm of the personal, he is simply not ready, he knows as much. His time has not come. But waiting and seeing is in itself a work, and a noble one. Compare the crank, who goes in for the specialty – of research, of verse, of politics, anywhere really that allows him, these days, to flaunt his liberty from the ordinary existence of homo mutabilis. "I do not need to change", the crank boasts. People may set him on a pedestal, they almost certainly will if he gives himself sufficient airs. And if he exudes intense self-appreciation, or charisma, he will be lauded as a holy man or perhaps as a guru. His fate will

5

be decided by those who play fast and loose with their illicit sensations and experiences of him as 'the specialist', 'the expert' in some field, or on some mountain, or perhaps in the Gobi.

The philosopher runs away from people's adulation and stands still only for their blame. He becomes still and quiet and immobile then. He knows it refines him, even during his time of anonymity. If they try to make him their king, he runs for the hills or, more likely, he automatically does something absurd, makes a fool of himself or speaks a harsh word. At the very moment of lending himself to society's confirmation he makes of himself either a laughing-stock or an object of disgust. The revealed crank has no such problem. His progress into the arms of society is smooth and wide. His relationship to society is extremely complicated; it would take a hundred pages to describe only a few of the typical and time-honoured networks of self-indulgence and deception that gradually harden, like a spaghetti junction, under the outward show of glamour and pomp. Overpasses and underpasses have to be added all the time until eventually the result is one big traffic snarl, but by then prestige is established and who knows enough to care by now about human communality under the exoskeleton, no, under the dead shell – of specialist popularity?

What about the philosopher's works, as he waits and sees?

There is above all the anonymous work of his individuality. "Here I stand" he says, "ready for this and that" and his hands might as well be in his pockets, for all the use he makes of them. Being alert and awake is work, because the human being naturally begins to slumber and snore if the central capacity for growth is not exercised with a perfectly free will, to whatever good end. The philosopher does wake-up work. He translates his tendency to unconsciousness into stimulating products. Eventually, he knows, there will be greater tasks for him to accomplish. Perhaps the has not yet learned the philosopher's tact, which prevents precipitation in a moral vacuum. Perhaps he has not yet come into the good habit of depending on his inner resources during times of dilemma or crisis. He might not be able to explain to his wife's satisfaction what he does all day, but when she doubts the validity of it he soon learns a few more devices. He waits. That prevents him from falling under the spell of the popular survival and prestige business. And he sees. He is conscious of himself in his neck of the woods, even though various forces operate to make him overlook his singularity and his distinction. He transforms these forces into potential faculties – into potencies, which he stores meanwhile. Now and again he falls asleep – and is forced then to experience a rude awakening. Or he rushes into some project that really has nothing to do with his present stage of growth, and then he burns his fingers or – sacrifices himself. No matter, that gets added on later.

This work of waiting and seeing, as we have said, may go on for years. Each work is a critique of a force or of a power that would either send him into a blind sleep or into precipitate action. How sorry we feel for him when suddenly we see him overrun or pushed against a wall by one of these. However we cannot help him. We are not philosophers. He has to find his own way. What can he do, to make it known to all and sundry that now he is ready for 'real action', whatever that is? Nothing. He will suddenly find himself acting in reality. The forces and powers have given up. He has proven that he can withstand the lot – of those that pertain to him, of course – and now he takes his hands out of his pockets. What do these hands of his represent?

Has he not a concerted effort to make now in the name of his humanity?

Not his individuality any more but his humanity interest him now. He steps forward, identifies the mysterious being and ... comes to terms with it. He gazes down on the world, on society, on his circle of acquaintances and friends and – he wishes them well. The critique is no longer necessary. Only the crank imagines he can rid the world of all enemies forever. The philosopher rids himself only of his own enemies – the enemies of vision and wakefulness and all the purveyors of a false rest. Now he envisions the rest per se. His work breathes a few life, originates in other spheres. Those who observe him detect a note of assurance. He is free to work or not to work, this is something quite new, immediately obvious in his behaviour. No longer does he take on an enemy but now he simply relies on the rest of reality. If he has managed to espouse a Christian tradition he might say that Jesus in his being carries him. He might keep quiet about this too, because he would not wish to be misunderstood on this score; to be classed with the church attenders and the sectarians.

Of course, as one would expect, there is a characteristic interim period of lassitude and depression. There are no more enemies – what can that mean? The persuasion is worthlessness. The true rest first has to become graphic and plastic. At first this philosopher is bound to still lack the appropriate respect. He still wants to pull at the cart but there is no more cart. His desires have vanished – what can that mean? Gently, like a bather into cold water, he lowers himself into the terrain that has been prepared for him. Nothing is to be done until he arrives there. He understands the theory of it by now, for he has plumbed the worthlessness and drunk deep of the lassitude, and this had taught him that a change is imminent. He steels himself for it, but it soon becomes plain to him that this particular change he cannot possibly meet halfway. The emphasis seems to be entirely on this business of his entrusting himself into that which he cannot identify or name. He has, in the past, become so accustomed to willing, that now he can barely come to terms with himself as someone whose willing is suspended and no longer relevant. He is bound to wonder: What will arrive in its stead? Is he to suffer? But that has in fact been the task of his will in the past when it gave in to pain and to death. When his will could no longer function, he suffered. Then, when he had suffered and undergone all there was to suffer and to undergo, he straightaway began to will again. Such were the natural ebbs and flows of his life's tide, the systole and diastole. Now he is to come into his reward. What is the philosopher's reward?

We have mentioned the rest of reality. Who can describe it? Right away something impersonal tends to block out the facts of the matter. We think of rest as rest *from*, and so the personal element is probably neglected or ignored. The rest we mean here works wonders. It is unthinkable without the personal element. In other words, someone else, or several others must be included in it, or better, must be entailed by it.

The philosopher shares his rest with several others – and this is his reward in truth, that he lives in community with several, and that these know him and acknowledge what stems from him. If he were to say now what his aim is he would point to these others and name them as the inheritors of his rest.

*

Do we say now that as the philosopher – or shall we say 'a' philosopher – nears the outwardly effective stage of his career he has no more will of his own? Or do we mean that he is no longer self-willed? Or that he is no longer liable to be self-willed? Does he now begin to say: "Not my will, but yours?" – and whom would he be addressing?

Our human will is a peculiar manifestation. It makes sense to speak of such a thing only in the case of someone who has not yet discovered the rest of reality.

Once I have discovered the rest of reality, then it is not my will, but I. How can I explain this to anyone who means his will when he says: "I"? Where he feels full of himself he will experience in me an emptiness. I in turn will see in him, when he speaks in his own name, something as yet not quite real. There cannot be any understanding or communication unless I allow for his will as something that actually stands in his way if

9

and while he tries to communicate with me and to understand me. It is I who must make the allowance.

For it is I, not he, who have discovered the true course of the so-called human will. I know what it means to have one's will broken and what it means to be self-willed, and I understand that neither of these is appropriate to personal growth. While I am self-willed I try to break the will of the other, to enslave him, and if my will is broken I automatically solicit the self-will of the other and tempt him to become a tyrant.

While we think of our will as an appetite, we may as well ask: an appetite for what? Is it not always an appetite chiefly for life and for an abundance of it? We may try to satisfy this appetite foolishly, greedily, anxiously or in any number of un-suitable ways, but what we are after is always more life and more variety of a manifold life. Then, when this comes, and when all the wrong attempts have failed and we have learnt from our failures and achieved the right one, the thirst is quenched and the hunger is stilled. Satisfaction sets in. Now we have to learn how to cope with that.

A philosopher at the end sets himself the task of learning how to cope with satisfaction. It may take him a while to come to terms with it. After all, his will is not to be involved. Neither will he be inclined to do the necessary. And yet something is to be done. It is not through not-doing that he will come to terms with total satisfaction and with the rest of reality. For the time being he takes care not to glance off either on the side of self-will or broken will, on the side of inclination or force. Some-thing nameless is coming his way and he is beginning to sense it. He does not wait for it. Neither does he reach out for it.

Then he knows that he has it.

So whenever in future dissatisfaction comes upon him, this is not because he must now attain to satisfaction but because he does not know that he is satisfied ... and then he knows it.

So the emphasis is on knowledge, and of course on the knowledge of knowledge, which is understanding.

The philosopher at the end of his career knows that he is satisfied, and he makes a point of knowing it. He cannot any more *be* dissatisfied, or incomplete, and whenever he *feels* that he is, among others or by himself, he knows this as a feeling and as something that does not coincide with reality. Then he corrects this by knowing that in truth and in reality he is complete and fulfilled. Then he *feels* fulfilled again too.

He is ready now to take on all challenges on this basis of his perfection, the appearance of which is correctible. Let us say that he is moved; right away he no longer feels complete. He corrects that appearance and immediately is in the possession of an efficient response. His works from now on proceed from every corrected position of completeness or perfection. His true speech originates in the rest of reality.

What is there left for him to do? Everything. The point is that now his task is to perfect and to complete. Whatever he touches reveals to him its own characteristic failing in terms of the whole. Whatever touches him leaves upon him the imprint of its present imperfection. This does not worry him because he has what it takes to sustain himself under any and all pressures and within any context.

He is able to know the perfection that is in him and the completeness that he personifies. He knows that he is always whole, though it may at times seem otherwise.

Every philosopher sets us this live example. While we know we are whole, and in order to correct appearances to the contrary, we influence the world in a way that is indisputably good. Our knowledge of ourselves as whole, in spite of appearances to the contrary, brings about untold blessings. Our speech will be wholesome, our behaviour helpful and our action creative.

When we speak of 'the philosopher' we have in mind not a particular person but a mythic creation and we do well to learn how to make use of such creations. We may, for example, think of the philosopher in ourselves, meaning the part of us that loves wisdom rather than foolishness. Consequently when we contemplate our own perfection we will not mistake something made by ourselves, such as our image or idea of ourselves, for what we are in truth. We are perfect in truth, while anywhere else the terms of perfection cannot apply. Prior to our discovery of the personal truth we do not know of our perfection, except perhaps as a concept or as an idea, but certainly not in reality. This is the same as saying that unless we know god we cannot know who or what we are and therefore we stray in the darkness, so that universal beneficial influences are misinterpreted by us as an unkind fate.

That we are whole, this may be experienced by us, however always through communication. We are whole as persons, not as individuals, and a person by definition exists in communication.

Finally, the philosopher does not interfere. He does not meddle with the world or attempt to improve it, or try to change its appearance. If he takes a hand in building huts or mending fences, he has ulterior motives. If he marries and raises a family he looks beyond that. On what is his eye trained at all times, whether he immerses himself in daily activity or withdraws from it?

On his human being. This he knows like none other. Here he has ample opportunity to bring all his capabilities into play. And he does so, always for the sake of those around him.

(Sept. 1995)

2
Early Reading Ability etc.

Very young children who read only haltingly are not necessarily 'slow'. We tend to make that wrong assumption only because we compare them to the average. In a cultural climate where the average is lauded, however, the exceptional child sometimes carries the symptoms of the collective. By that I mean to say that what the many must neglect in order to appear conventionally alright asserts itself, negatively of course, in certain individual cases. If certain organs are not addressed by a developing society, for example, then those very organs are found to cause problems dysfunctionally in some who then exist, due to such dysfunction, near the edge of that society. Rather than the term community, the term society applies here. We are looking at phenomena as they appear at a level of consciousness but not in any awareness. We can speak of an organism called society, of the health of that organism, of the way certain parts of it look outwardly splendid while being inwardly hollow, and of other aspects that appear to be ailing in themselves, while in fact they signal a distress of the organism in general. The general health of that organism can therefore be diagnosed in the particular, through those edge phenomena.

On the surface it would appear now that the health of society can be improved by curing unsocial elements and by cutting off anti-social elements. Nothing could be further from the truth. The difficulty in this lies in the difference between consciousness and awareness, and in the fact that consciousness does not suffice for the purpose of perception in awareness. Society, the political state, certain popular institutions – these are organisms of consciousness. The arise in the first place as products of consciousness, and consciousness suffices to comprehend them in that light.

The light of awareness is brighter. In it, organisms appear to the eye as above described. Edge phenomena can now be clearly seen as symptomatic carriers of a burden due to collective excess or neglect. Organisms are fully understood now as not quite real and consciousness alone is apprehended, in perspective, as not the full story. Characteristic human-natural perception proceeds in awareness.

In the light of awareness we may perceive clearly the various assumptions that are made in the comparative half-light of consciousness. We notice how the stateless Jew is rejected by the State, how the unorthodox Christian is excommunicated by the Church, how the clinically diagnosed victim of insanity is sectioned into an asylum, the criminal becomes an object of corporate vengeance and – the child with poor reading ability is classed abnormal and given remedial attention so that in time he might read as well as the rest. Similarly, the Jews finally too have their State, unorthodoxy is no longer castigated by a 'tolerant' Church and the 'insane' are sent out into the Community. (I capitalize so as to identify objects of consciousness in the light of awareness.)

However, as we mentioned earlier, organisms cannot be cured. An organism is by definition something that exists in the half-light of consciousness and can therefore not appear except with all the symptoms due to that half-light. There is no such thing as a healthy, sane, morally integrated organism. These terms cannot apply. If one finds that they are applied, then one does well to be sceptical of their meaning. Similarly, a 'sick society' is a pleonasm.

*

The creative, and only morally justifiable, approach to an organism is therefore the following. One identifies the edge phenomena with their symptoms and undertakes a program of renewal. This is easily enough said, but alas! A magician or a miracle worker would be stumped. Those few who are aware of even the possibility of such renewal cannot help but sense how they themselves must always and on every occasion set the example of renewal. Impulses of recreative love are indispensable. Those who do not know how to suffer need not apply.

14

Take the pupil who has been diagnosed as 'in need of remedial attention'. Is he a victim of the standard education system? Is he being asked for a performance that goes against his natural grain? Are his difficulties of the type that could be described as symptomatic of undernourishment and malnutrition in terms of spirit? If so, then we might say that difficulties with reading, for example, are a sign of that and, at the same time, an opening through which the missing food can be introduced. The chief aim then would not be to get that child to read but to introduce him to the light of awareness and to familiarize him very gradually with some aspect of himself or the world in that light. A way of achieving that end might be remedial help with his reading. I say: 'might be' because other opportunities for arriving at the same goal might present themselves and then, coincidentally, the problem with reading disappears.

*

It seems odd that our children should learn how to read. Ordinarily intelligent mothers declare proudly that their seven year old sons and daughters have 'the reading ability of a sixteen-year-old'. We have forgotten how reading and writing fit into the human natural scheme of things. Writing is a craft which can be turned into an art. Adults have their own will-power consciously at their disposal, so that human nature may, in that adult, choose to contemplate itself, which results every time in such a joyous occasion that life nearly demands to be communicated. So, for example, an adult speaks, while children talk. The living spoken word is an adult comprehension and an aim for children, set in front of them by parental adults. Why should a child wish to write? The written word itself testifies to a joyous overflowing of human nature for the purpose of communion. Children cannot experience such a need for communion. So what children learn is not to write but to scribble. They do not learn to read but to imitate sounds. They are schooled in the habits of immature adults, and when they themselves become adults they have the immaturity ready made for them implanted in their brains. Not that I expect anyone to believe or accept this, but it wants to be said and I intend to oblige it. Modern society has decided in its wisdom that infants, if possible, should be able to read, and precocity is a marvel. Early reading ability is not scoffed at but admired.

What I am suggesting, perhaps with too much of the force of a sledgehammer, is that we are treating our children as though they were monkeys, and that if a child refuses to be treated like that, and if his organic being is in some department revolting against such treatment, this may well be a refreshing sign of primal humanity, and backwardness only in comparison to all those trained monkeys. Imagine a number of generations becoming skilled in walking on their hands and then suddenly comes along an upstart child who will either walk on his feet or break out in a rash all over his body.

A great deal of what has been admired as art through the ages amounts to an immature hammering of human nature, and the magic that is looked for in art is really a symptom of revolt. Indeed for how long has not 'nature' meant everything else except 'human nature'?

Of course a child can be taught to translate letters into sounds or sounds into letters. Or rather, he cannot be taught this, because teaching is not involved, only training. Now toilet training is useful, and eating with cutlery if the cutlery is clean. But how can the alphabet make sense to children? An apple makes sense, or a game of hide and seek. Then the parental adult's behaviour makes sense if that adult is mature; but no kind of immaturity, such as foisting on a child speech and behaviour patterns that have long since died the death of hypocrisy, can impress a child favourably.

At fifteen or sixteen years of age children would be just about old enough to learn how to read and write, because now they could actually learn it and not just imitate copies of a semblance. They could actually learn it now because they are beginning to make contact with their conscious and intentional desires. And how quickly they would learn it, if their brains had not previously been taxed to exhaustion with monkey-tricks! We can learn to speak when we have something to say, but if someone tries to make us speak before that, he will only succeed in defeating our willingness to talk.

Society will continue to train children as though they were monkeys, and we ourselves will make our own admirable contribution to this to the extent of our own dependence on society. But to some it will occur that Society is an organism, and that therefore anything of a societal origin should not be confused with human nature or reality. Even those few who are willing to understand this will still continue to make societal judgments, in spite of themselves and on account of the training and schooling they received as children – but they will chide themselves for it and seek forgiveness. Happily human nature is eminently forgiving, especially once we have made a good habit of giving a degree of mature thought to our adult ability to do as we wish and to wish as we do. The dynamics of the universal originality at our disposal may actually be discovered by each one of us in a relatively painless way, but we must not expect to be thanked and rewarded for it by Society, since Society recognizes nothing except what appears in the half-light of consciousness. Once we become aware of Society we are bound to opt for community; we can nearly not help it. We search in the heart of the person next to us for common humanity and we proffer our own. Our existence becomes a series of open secrets and happy surprises.

*

To a creative adult, with a fingertip sensitivity for human nature in all its artful guises and protective disguises, precocity in a child is nowhere near as exciting, to say the least, as so-called backwardness. More often than not what is admired as precocity in a child is a combination of childish vanity with a knack for animal imitation, or aping. The childish mind can be sufficiently seduced, by individuals or by the cultural milieu, to appear as genius. Since Society does not differentiate between mere appearances and true appearance, such children are sometimes doomed to 'success'. The so-called genius is such a highly questionable phenomenon, mirroring not only in works but even in self the ambiguity of Society as a final state. Again, such phenomena are interesting as symptoms, to those with the right sort of compassion. Of course the whole business can be seen as one of human nature's survival tricks under the pressure of a collective short-sightedness. But our main energy must go not into interpretation but towards amelioration. How do we deal with backwardness, unwillingness, downright rebelliousness in a child? How do we approach the abnormality, the peculiarity, the handicap, the disability and the dysfunction? Do we try to make the child fit in with conventional prejudice and traditionally entrenched bias and hypocrisy, or do we search for the human child in pain, for the individual child not yet compassionately addressed, for youthful human nature in search of maturity and freedom? If the latter, then we are obliged to become aware of the sheer inappropriateness of the goals and aims sanctioned by Society and honoured by the State. We waste no time judging or condemning these, but we learn to listen wherever true human nature cries for help and then we respond with our own, spontaneously, so that intelligence, insight and active choice are organically founded. Morally we have to be twice as inventive as our selfish chicanes. If we do not take evil into account, first and foremost in ourselves, we end up duped by it.

How delightful, on the other hand, to make progress in the direction of creativity, where burdens are eased, existence is verified and living becomes a pleasure! Children today are to learn to read as early as possible, that seems to be the law. Those who can approach this predicament, and the anguish that sometimes arises because of it, in the light of true awareness can help bring on the time when such a 'law', or custom, will no longer be necessary. Meanwhile help individual children in pain.

(Sept. 95)

3

Instant Gratification of the Intellect

The desire to learn is a spiritual growth impulse. Once we begin to grow spiritually, however early in our time of life, we develop this appetite for knowledge and understanding. Observe it in children, how they long for the discovery of this and of that, and how long it takes for their eager approach to the world to be thwarted. The spirit of most children is so lively for news that it must be misled down several dead-end avenues before it finally resigns itself to cynicism or cold ambition. education should begin by liberating children from these, not by confirming them.

But what sort of a thing do we mean, in general, when we speak of our intellect? In our day and age, intellect bears a myriad connotations. Mental activity we think of as intellectual, especially if removed from the physical. We call someone an intellectual if his mental activity has in a strange way become self-sufficient. He reminds us of the fox in the fable, who through negligence has lost his tail and then tries to persuade the rest of the tribe that being tailless is nicer. The intellectual has acquired a kind of crippling self-sufficiency, in which he alone takes a blind pride. It helps him to an extent if he is surrounded by his own kind.

If we ask what has gone wrong with 'the intellectual' we assume that he abuses this faculty of intellection in himself, and that ultimately he abuses himself and others. We also imply that we know of some more life-like use of this faculty.

If we, as human beings, like to learn because through learning we grow, then surely this learning-faculty must be placed by us at the service of that which we hope to learn. We do not use it like a stick, to beat something into submission, so that it will do us slave-duty, nor do we make of it a pattern into which something has to fit before we will have anything to do with it.

Since intellection is growth, and growth is towards something greater than ourselves, it would seem that a spirit of humility is essential. What we know and understand at the moment is usually rounded off in some way, almost as if that were all that was to it. A sort of complacency seems unavoidable after every quantum of knowledge, and then we get a natural reminder, of the painful kind, that growth continues, whereupon we do well to become intellectually active so as to recreate the bridge, from what we already know to what is still new. This bridge should extend from the finite to the infinite, from the familiar to the unknown, from the thing we can manage and handle to that which as yet has no handle, so we cannot even pick it up.

The properly useful intellectual attitude therefore keeps us soberly in mind of our present limitations while we invite the as yet unlimited.

Of course we must have some notion of this unlimited, endless ... what ... shall we call it our medium? Or our environment? We must have heard of that which is greater than ourselves, beyond which we cannot possibly grow, otherwise we are lost. It takes time, tradition and application, as a matter of fact, to bring a human being to the point where he assumes that all has been figured out, whereupon he cannot help but despise it, since growth for him has stopped, so that degeneration and perversion have set in. Out of this deplorable state of affairs he must be educated – but not according to some system of education which acknowledges only and exclusively the finite, thus giving it a bad name. The intellectual is the fish out of water. Our intellect is like the gills of the fish.

Traditionally the name given to that which is infinite and unlimited is spirit. Any attempt to represent or imagine spirit as such must fail, because we would then be presenting the unlimited as finite, the endless as bound. We would be defeating our own purpose while trying to achieve it.

But then this is just fine, because spirit is not to be represented or imagined but to become incarnate. Spirit longs or desires to become incarnate, to marry with flesh. Indeed we know about spirit precisely because of this longing or desire with which we are suddenly in touch and to which we may respond, though we are at liberty to resist it. Initially this notion of such a thing as spirit stems from experience. We can abstract from this unique desire or longing everything that can be abstracted, all form and content, all that is perceivable and measurable, and still – there it is. "Right," we way. "Call it spirit." Never let it be said that spirit is an idea, Ideas are impossible in the absence of spirit. If, however, we have never been touched by spirit or experienced this unique longing which so strangely imparts itself to us, then we may well be ... but this thought is impossible. The fact of the matter is that all have at least been touched by spirit, there is no way around that. Where we differ is in whether or not we respond, and in the nature and degree of our response.

Now it happens that if we set out to apprehend and to comprehend spirit we proceed intellectually and intelligently. This activity is initially head-work but our heart is involved. A moment or two ago we spoke of humility as a crucial context for learning, and this humility is an involvement of our heart. So the head initiates while the heart obliges. Genuine intellectual progress can be observed from two sides like this. The cleverness of the head in tandem with the humility of the heart, while the head does the steering.

21

Now here is where some people go badly wrong because they say: "I am ready with the head and with the heart, but I see no spirit on which to work or against which to apply myself." The simple secret of the matter is: If the head is intact and the heart is ready, here is spirit. Spirit is absent only because head and heart are not yet up to the mark. They must be prepared, and spirit is absent only because of insufficient preparation. Really this preparation should more specifically be called intellectual work. Once spirit has come into it we ought to describe this as intelligence. Intellect allows us to cope with the experience of spiritual longing and desire, while intelligence then accommodates actual spirit as incarnate.

But the difference between intellect and intelligence is not so important for us here as what we do sometimes when we do not want to take the time for the preparation, in acknowledgment of spirit as greater than ourselves (or at least as never smaller or less than ourselves) but we behave as though we might impress our own will and desire on spirit, to make it do our bidding. Instead of letting patience do its work, we lose patience and insist – on instant gratification of that longing. We become intellectually presumptuous. Not that anyone can say how long it should take, what we have in mind to achieve during this preparation, but that we wrongly suppose we can dispense with time altogether, this is what makes us immature and presumptuous.

The fact that intellection takes time is often overlooked because the longing of spirit, which can also be called the longing for spirit, is so intense and the desire so strong. Time has become a modern impediment, when it should be seen as the pace of reality. Good spirit is always available for our intellection, but if we get it wrong, if we mistake that longing or desire, we end up with bad spirit. Any time we choose we an long for good spirit and just then we have it, this has to be said, in case anyone supposes we have to wait for an experience of spirit as longing. Such an experience is usually necessary at the start so that we should become more dissatisfied with ourselves as orphans from spirit, but thereafter we may desire as we wish, for we are aware of the spirit's reality, having been touched by it and able to remember that.

Such an intentional and voluntary longing for good spirit cannot go wrong because intellection originates in such cases from head and heart in unison, so that thought and humility are joined. But where willing and thinking go on at the same time, no time is lost because we have all the time in the world. It is in the area and within the context of that initiatory experience of spirit as longing or desire that intellection goes awry, so that preparation for good spirit remains insufficient and intellectualism occurs, as an indulgence in bad spirit.

The practical institution of intellect is the only antidote to intellectualism. This must begin with a desire for the truth, and perhaps with a radical desire for the truth. While we desire the truth we are not to be swayed by any mistaken desires or longings, such as may have emerged due to our misconception or sheer ignoration of inspired longings and desires.

We sometimes forget that the ability to think something through is a characteristic of maturity and that thought training can liberate us from immaturity. But immaturity is a lack of response, a wrong attitude or a bad reaction to spirit. We can tackle immaturity quite satisfactorily in terms of our intellectual capacity for thinking and learning. And it helps if we realize that immaturity sets in as soon as we hasten to a satisfaction of our mental appetites rather than first soliciting sponsorship of the truth in our hearts, or in our breast, or however we like to imagine it. A hasty reaction is far from a response. It may be understandable as being born out of the fear of missing out where an ill-conceived longing pictures a myriad rewards, but anything born out of fear is destructive, all the more so if it sets itself up constitutionally as a body of sorts. It may also be seen as the seed-bed of spiritual pride, where a legitimate spirit impulse is aborted in favour of mischievous or nefarious gain.

The true thinking and learning process, or intellection, is not born out of fear but out of an intentional and voluntary love of the truth, which implies an overcoming of all that stands in the way of a perfectly peaceful spirit influence. If our spiritual appetite is for self-gratification, for pleasing others or our selves, then we must first turn this around so that it becomes an appetite for the truth, and this is our mature responsibility, though it may seem demeaning, embarrassing and generally inglorious. Always the truth appears negligible, until the time comes when we know it, and then we understand how far we were off the mark.

There is no reason why our intellect should not be instantly gratified. Why should we not immediately turn to the peaceful spirit of truth and gain the satisfaction of our desire? Why should the desire to learn and the longing for wisdom not right away be met? There is no reason why it should not. The simple fact is, that we are no up to it. The simple down-to-earth truth is that when we are touched by the spirit that is good we flinch. We react. Momentarily we rebel. If we are to grow, to live and not to die, then we are urged from within and stimulated from without. The urgency goes to the head. The stimulus overwhelms. We need to be able to cope with rushes of passion and with mental set-backs, and those who never hate or feel guilty have probably never taken on the shortcomings of the person next to them. Compassion implicates, humility lays us open to ridicule and action risks error. The one who said: "Whatever you do in my name is bound to do you good," had precisely these liabilities of ours in mind. Through him then we may have instant gratification of our intellect, but this only raises the objection of all those around us who refuse to know him, whose burden we share. Once again we run the risk of intellectual exclusiveness by forming or joining a Religion. Once again we rush to the conclusion that those who belong are better than those outside, and those who disagree with us must be wrong. Or we swear by the one who carries our burden while we remain half-hearted.

Intellect reaches within us to the depth of our being and draws us to our highest aspirations. An immense gap separates those who wish to learn and grow from those who prefer to survive. Our anguish concerns those who have not learnt that they have what they request, so they reach out beyond themselves and lose their equilibrium, and then they call that good. Spirit seems nowhere so unforgiving as when we intend to coerce it, so that our intellect becomes an instrument of torture while human nature is stretched on the rack. Remember that learning means leaving ourselves open to the influence of reality under circumstances that do not always seem favourable.

4

What is Hope?

Certainly I hope to be able to answer this question in one of an infinite number of possible ways within ten (manuscript) pages, specifically for once as an antidote, as the antidote, to depression. It will be interesting to see what we can learn about it under these auspices.

Depression can be brought on by a heavy meal. Also, it is a heavy meal. It is a word from the mouth of god and we might do worse than learn how to digest it. This is different from keeping it at bay. Personally I see no reason for trying to keep it at bay, though that does not mean that I go in for heavy meals, as a rule. The sailor likes the wind to blow, but that does not mean that he sows it.

So I start this little treatise at the very beginning of a bout of depression. Let it be a hopeful treatise. Let it demonstrate what it preaches.

I propose to be able to come up with hope, to be hopeful, on occasion and demand, and I am suggesting here that a most suitable occasion is the beginning, the very first small whiffs, of a depression. From one sentence to the next I find myself stopped, arrested in my tracks, depressed, with only one way out and forward: hope. Everything is wiped out, all tracks, all signs, and all that is left is that notorious sinking feeling, that sensation of being swallowed by a hippopotamus of a cloud. Of course I am grateful for being able to describe it. My gratitude is strongly allied to what I mean by hope. In other words I am grateful at this moment in time for being able to tackle this depressive onset digestively. My stomach is involved. Hope has its gastric origins. It helps to know that, in case we go for our brain exclusively. A hopeless man has little appetite. He tries to stimulate himself out of his depression by eating anchovies or pâtés, but very of likely he is already overloaded in that area, the area of 'bread alone', so he only makes matters worse. Stimulation is no antidote to depression at all. We stimulate our appetite, but if our method of satisfying appetite has become narrow, often narrow to the extreme, we need to branch out and get away from the dinner table entirely. We are over-stimulated and over-satisfied, but within extremely narrow limitations. The question is how to get away from this enthralment, from this dependency on one single satisfaction. We may have read books to the exclusion of every other activity. When the unavoidable depression sets in, why try to stimulate our interest in life through reading?

The ability to hope, as the ability to think or to feel, whenever one chooses, is, of course, human through and through, and in no way popular. The spirit of voluntary awareness resides in human beings and not in people. We do not, for example, have to ask: 'What does it feel like?' before we can commence to hope. On the other hand, we know that there are ways of being fully and wholly human that work automatically, and we only need to wish to support them to be in the way of them, or on them. We can call them virtues. Virtues are ways of being wholly human. Hope is one of them. No one can be wholly human unless he does it in one way or another, this has to be recognized, so that we get away from such notions as ideal or pure humanity on earth. In the mind yes, but not on terra firma.

Interesting, but after all not surprising, that we should come up with hope as a virtue on the basis of a depression. On the basis of it? Hardly. How could a depression support anything? And yet, while we seriously consider the possibility and reality of hope, that depression does work like a support, like something we can kick off from, at least. "But a moment ago you spoke in terms of digestion. Now you move in the realm of mechanics. Is that still wise?"

"We have moved on since then. Depression can be all-pervasive, you now that fine well. The digestive approach can be most readily remembered and instigated at such a crucial time. At the start we only know the experience of the stupor, of that running sore called despair. People get so depressed that they kill themselves, and nobody can help them. Human beings at least have a way out, but the thing has to be learned. Choose your own metaphors if you dislike mine. I must warn you, I may come up with a third one before I finish."

There are other virtues. Let's not quarrel about that. The times are over when we need to categorize programmatically. People have no idea what we are talking about here and they are not very likely to make it their business. If you want to discuss fully human behaviour you may as well give it a name. We live among people and there is a reason for that. I has to do with learning how to be fully and wholly human. A fully human being is virtuous. Please forget about the moral implications of virtuous being. A whole human being must be human in some way, on terra firma, among others. What is the use of pretending that a human being could exist in someone's mind?

I myself at the moment am hopeful. I want to be hopeful, and I trust that the skill for it is in me. It is in me inasmuch as I want to be at home in the perfect order of beings and things. I do of course believe that such a perfect order exists. Reality, so far as I am concerned, is perfect, and I don't care who believes me. Imperfections are not part of reality. No matter how much of a failure I feel, how much of a demon or dunce, that takes nothing away from the existence in the light of day right here and now of perfect reality. Look for it. You will find it. To what should I compare it? A man went forth from his home and family because he imagined he was dying and he did not wish to inflict the spectacle on his nearest and dearest. They had, in any case, grown remote from him, and were not so dear to him any more at all. The fresh air in the mountains, the clear, clean water, the brilliant horizons had an effect on him and soon he wanted to live. In retrospect, as he now thought, he had not at all wanted to live, he had only taken life as it came and when it had faltered he had caved in. There would be no more of that. He visited a hermit in a cave and told him of his discovery. "I can choose to live," he said. "What do you think of that?" The hermit right away made detailed enquiries. The two became friends. They travelled for a while and then they came to the fertile plain on the other side of the mountains. There they parted company again and each went his own way. Eventually our friend arrived back at his home where his wife and children had not aged at all. They had not even noticed that he was away. Often he laughed when he thought about this experience, and when his wife asked him why he was laughing he always made up a new reason, and always he took the opportunity to explain that he was happy, and this helped to make her more happy too. They live on and on now, because they choose to do so. And this is really the case.

The next thing we have to take into consideration is that hope, like any other human virtue, can become habitual. While you experience depression, hope is not yet habitual, and the depression is like an invitation to you to hope and to learn how to do it. You might as well look forward to your next depression, instead of worrying about it. People fear depression. Human beings look for special opportunities to hope. I just want you to be clear about the difference. If not hope, then some other virtue. Once a virtue has become habitual we call it life.

So technically we do not choose to hope in order to get out of another depression but so as to have more life. It is a common mistake, to try to be virtuous for the sake of admiration or so as to feel better. Neither is virtue its own reward. Eventually life is the reward, and for the sake of life, eventually, we learn, and practice, and habituate our virtues.

But now how is hope different from other virtues, tell us that. Name another one, for a start.

Work is another virtue. Think of work as a combination of courage and strength. Be strong and have courage, and that means you work. I don't say <u>feel</u> strong, but <u>be</u> strong. You can be strong while you are feeling weak. Just as you can have courage while you feel like and look like a coward.

Hope when you are depressed. When should you work?

Especially when you are afraid and weak. If you wish to work then, you will learn what it means to work. Of course I do not mean work for money or for prestige. And when you are scared and weak you feel least like work, like doing anything except running and hiding. Nevertheless, here is the opportunity for laying in more life by developing and habituating another virtue. As I mentioned above, virtues gradually become more habitual and less explicit. As hope and work become more habitual they become less distinguishable as virtues. As your humanity broadens and deepens you will be less frequently depressed, scared and weak, and your hoping and working will have become less distinguishable from living. Eventually you won't need people around you any more and the company of human beings will be much more to your taste. One would think, by the way, that human beings automatically prefer one another's company to that of people, but this is not so, because human beings emphasize and accentuate in one another their own shortcomings and imperfections, I mean by their sheer presence to one another. So often human beings prefer the company of people, because here they can, for a time only, indulge their imperfections – to popular applause. But suddenly things turn bad, and then that human being is much further behind than if he had worked with human beings. But of course it is silly to try to avoid people. Take them as you find them and then let them go again. That suffices for you to become aware of your need for various virtues and you have a ready supply of raw materials for building your human house.

You see, I have need of that third metaphor now. You digest the depression, you push off from it, and now you use it as raw materials, for building. Every virtue can be tackled in those three ways. I find that reassuring. The house you build is your human security and confidence.

I find it rather amusing that these human virtues are distinguishable in terms of the undesirable states that precede them, not in terms of some object that is attained by them or some change that is brought about by them. If you want to know what hope in itself is, you have to look to the depressing despair that suggests it as a useful virtue to acquire. The habitual virtue is indistinguishable from life. Hoping and working become more and more like living. When a human being first sets out to distinguish himself, he begins to live in a small way, though his smallest human life is greater than the greatest popular life. As he practices his various virtues, his life becomes richer, more manifold; his living becomes more effective and powerful.

Let him not shun other human beings but love them. Soon he learns to distinguish between human beings and people. He likes people because they are like him. Human beings present him with the sort of challenge and threat that can only be dealt with successfully if he loves them. Let him cultivate a high regard for other human beings, though he may find their company initially threatening and inconvenient. Human beings are very much in the minority. He loves them more effectively the more life he can give them. The life he gives to them, by loving them, he gets back manifold. People he likes or dislikes and he leaves it at that. He neither shuns the ones he dislikes nor does he particularly seek out the ones he likes. From that direction come the raw materials for his constructive activities.

Hope is a virtue and virtues are tributaries into eternal life. Hope is that particular virtue which grows as we digest, oppose or use up depression and despair. You will know when the time for hope has come because you will feel hopeless. Despair is the state of utter hopelessness, and depression is the beginning of that state. Grasp every opportunity to hope. Do not offload your despair onto others. Be too ambitious and too clever for that. Do you not want the life that comes as habitual hope? Would you really rather die?

(24/12/'95)

5

Pain and the Active individual

Examine yourself. Where does it hurt? Nowhere? You are either dead or sinking into destruction. You might also be rising into destruction. My contention is, that any live human being must be able, at any given moment, to point to a pain in himself, in his flesh, his soul or his body. A whole, or healed human being knows that the pain he carries is someone else's burden that has been laid on him and now he can get to work. Any time he chooses he can take the quantum of pain accumulated until then, since last he worked, and fashion something useful, something helpful to those who could in all fairness be called the authors or origins of his pain.

There are not very many whole human beings around. All too many still need to be healed. Their attitude towards pain, towards inconvenience and discomfort, towards sickness and loneliness, is usually ambivalent. When they run away from it or repress it they feel ashamed of themselves and when they suffer it after a fashion they feel guilty. Strung out between shame and guilt, modern human beings, who are not whole, arbitrate day in day out between these two affects, because they quite rightly suspect that neither of them should cause them trouble.

There is not a single human being, modern or otherwise, who does not wish to distinguish himself. I do not mean distinguish himself as a personality among people but as a whole human being, singular and unique in his own right, with his own unrepeatable contribution to make to the perfect order of beings and things in reality. This wish is discernible even in some very young children. Every experience of pain is to facilitate this distinction, so that the human being will know his individuality, on one hand, rather than turning into a herd animal, and, on the other hand, so that he will turn into a person and not into an individual. So much for the science of pain. It exists for a reasonable purpose which may always again, on every occasion of pain, be understood afresh, so that growth towards distinction may come about as naturally as possible.

The growth towards distinction cannot be divorced from what we do in the interest of our distinction. Any worthwhile perception of pain takes into account the fact that growth and activity go hand in hand. Modern human beings do not comprehend this and consequently they are strung out between guilt and shame. Stunted growth and wild growth, presumptuous activity and thwarted activity, all these are affected as guilt and shame.

How we perceive pains, and that we suffer them, both of these are of crucial importance. I cannot suffer a heartache

32

unless I realize that something worthwhile in terms of life, such as a greater capacity of compassion perhaps, stands at the end of the suffering process. The suffering must be goal oriented towards life if it is to go on in a worthwhile manner. But suffering may also simply facilitate growth, in the direction suggested by that pain, by that anxiety or by that back ache. Why should our suffering not be joyful, If we know fine well, as we do, that something immensely worthwhile must be coming our way? This joy makes the suffering easy.

We look at this physiology complex from the other side and come face to face with the active individual. We mean to include the passive individual. He suddenly arises in us and makes his presence felt. We might speak of a spirit, of a spiritual entity, as long as we keep in mind that this spirit is demonic and not good. We do well to identify it as soon as possible. The longer we entertain it, the more do we squander our ability to suffer, and this ability should be precious to us.

The thing to do with this spirit is simply to shun it and to get it behind us. It is blind to the need for suffering in the interest of life. It would council the avoidance of suffering and the suppression of pain as though there were no such thing. It sets itself above every experience of pain, and it manages to do this by acting out energy. When a given supply of energy has been acted out, this spirit disappears and leaves us gasping for breath, devoid of compassion and poorer in ability to suffer. We complain of a lack of energy. We should suffer the pain of feeling wasted. Instead we hanker for the stimulant of affective energy. We should wish for distinction. Instead we have tired ourselves out, allowed ourselves to become fatigued; we have sacrificed our peace and rest to this demon who can do absolutely nothing for the benefit of human beings and now we complain because we are not being rewarded. No intended reward fills the bill. We suspect ourselves of having somehow missed the boat and we suspect others of taking unfair advantage of us. In short, we experience guilt and shame. These can of course be suffered, each in its own right, as legitimate pains, but usually we are far too distracted or abusive to even think of such a thing. We then are liable to become unconscious, to fall asleep. Afterwards we feel refreshed and – full of energy, perhaps. Quick as a flash the active individual moves in and expects to be entertained by us, so that we ourselves should lend our body and soul, and become, for a period of time, active individuals instead of working and growing human beings. The passive individual is merely the luxuriating version of the active one. He likes to inhibit energy, to test himself against it as an inhibiting factor. Learn to recognize both the active and the passive aspect of this bad spiritual entity. Shun both, by shunning the one.

By practicing a thoroughgoing hygiene of our senses we make it difficult for this active, energetic individual, who worships industry, to take hold in us. All individuals are essentially in flight before the soiled eye; their own. They may be in flight on their legs or on their backs. Those who prefer passivity get others to do their dirty work for them.

We manage the hygiene of our senses with water and with fire. The passion and the action are both represented. Imagine you have an argument with someone. You come up with a few lucky opinions. They slip out of your hands. You feel tempted to make up for this apparent defeat by insisting on a conviction. It happens to be a natural enough temptation. But before you get properly stuck in, it occurs to you to honour your opponent's conviction. This amounts to the hygiene of your sense of justice; to an instance of it. Essentially you honour your opponent; is his conviction not at bottom a self-identification?

Or your child needs to be told to do this or that. You could do it more quickly and efficiently yourself, but he needs the discipline of intelligent occupation. You notice the look on his face when you tell him what to do. You feel tempted to change your mind, angrily or indulgently. Instead you join him in the activity, you make it a little more bearable for him. This amounts to a cleansing of your sense of fair play. Again you replaced a perfectly natural temptation with a perfectly human act, in both cases an act of mercy, and the result was that you were able to see clearly, to sense profoundly, and were therefore able to avoid the active/passive individual, who would otherwise have possessed you – to neglect your parental privilege in the latter case and to dishonour the bonds of friendship in the former.

One pain leads to another. What counts is that we know why we suffer, and that our reason for suffering is more life and richer life. Sorrow, distress, a toothache – every day comes along with its portion of pain. We do well to keep up. If we get behind, we are faced with the problem of suffering ten years' pain. No one should ever have to do that. But it can be done. Catch up as soon as you can.

Suffering pain is part of living, just as the mixing of the pigments is part of painting. We have to overcome our wrong perceptions of pain and suffering. We want to be at ease on the earth, not racked by doubts or driven by a bad conscience. We have to get this business of suffering down to a fine art. When you talk to people about suffering, they suppose you mean being in pain and so they naturally suspect that the entire individual is taken over. They know how pain usurps the consciousness, so anyone who does not preach the flight from pain must mean unconsciousness and death. Since they have no awareness they cannot imagine how anyone can suffer and live. And the thought of suffering in order to really live, and to live more abundantly, must remain quite foreign to them. We should not attempt to instruct them. Instruction is for those who are naturally endowed.

The active individual sets in, in the place of such a natural endowment. Cautious observation allows us to discover the link between potential awareness and hectic business. Where the blind commotion begins to take over, there a truthful motivation has become a possibility. Think of it as a distinct possibility, either in the case of yourself or of another. The distinct possibility of awareness is, so to speak, trodden underfoot by the active individual. Here an opportunity for rescue work presents itself to the compassionate person. Ah well, he supposes, if only that demon could be stopped, a taste for the truth might rise to the surface, might enter consciousness. But in this he is somewhat wide of the mark. To stop a demon means to increase his energy. To confront a demon means to confirm him in his being. Then of course it would take the highest possible power of recognition to cast him out. A specifically gifted person can do this. The ordinary compassionate person defers to the demon and infers the capacity for awareness. Such a compassion amounts to a polite no with the left hand and a friendly yes with the right. The politeness is crucial, otherwise the active individual feels challenged in his rights. Any compassionate person will be naturally polite to any active individual. One senses that where this demon has taken an interest there must be something worthwhile after the nature of humanity. Demons crave to possess humanity. (We must try to apprehend this term 'demon' quite dispassionately. Socrates knew his demon. Jesus drove demons out.) So we remain open to the humanity, which we do by demonstrating a readiness to suffer the pain which is being energetically ignored by the individual, while at the same time we do not contend with that individual's rights to his individuality. This can be talked about in so many different ways. A compassionate person without individuality is unthinkable. It is precisely the fact that our individuality has gone astray that turns us into individuals, at the expense of communicating personality. An individual is not a person. I can tell that I have turned into an individual when I feel full of myself, only apparently distinct but in reality extinct. It flatters my nerves for a time, this extinction, and if ill luck would have it there will be some of those around me who will flatter me in my extinction and I will be led even further astray. I will, perhaps, turn into a personality. It feels wonderful, temporarily, when extinction and decay come together like this, and hopefully I will notice sooner or later what is going on and practice contrition, if possible with a cheerful heart and glad enough to be ashamed of myself. In this way I can find my way back to my human being.

The demon has no right to human being, but he does energetically pretend to it. How do we bind him, this strong man? By demonstrating our compassion for the afflicted human being. This is the rescue work we may undertake, and it involves no direct combat with the active individual. Remember, there is no need for him if the pain is suffered. The fear of pain invites him in. Suffering obviates fear of pain. Compassion is a demonstration of the fact that pain can be suffered, which is to say, that pain can be correctly understood as a pointer in the direction of personal action and growth. We can see here what it means to suffer for someone. Not the pain itself, but the fearful reaction to it, the anxiety and distress, is transferred to us, so that we then feel tempted to become energetic individuals, and instead we extend our compassion to the anxious person, to the one in whom the energetic individual is coming to the fore, and we show him by our example that the pain he fears can be suffered towards life.

(27/12/'95)

6

The Will to Suffer

Of course there can be no such thing as the will to suffer, because the two exclude each other. All the same such a thing is supposed to exist, and therefore attempted – or perhaps the other way around, it is attempted and therefore one supposes it must exist. The latter is more likely the case, because we happen into it, rather than undertaking it on sober reflection.

If we sicken of our will, upon much and a lengthy attachment to it, we want rid of it, we would like to try its antithesis. All our willed ambitions have turned out so wrong, so disappointing and hurtful, that we have quite enough now and we say: "I will the opposite of my will now, I will suffer," without realizing that this kind of suffering is only another mask of our will – of course. This is far too obvious not to miss.

But let's consider what we mean by will? Namely our impression on the world and our control of it. All these representations of things that we have come up with until now, consciously or accidentally, all the same whether we did it ourselves or blandly repeat what others did, they have given us a singular sense of satisfaction, of progress, and most of all perhaps, of worthiness. It worked for a while and then the joy went out of it.

I mean the way our will was defined by, and derived from, the world. And it returned the compliment. It, in turn, defined and made the world, out of gratitude and necessity. Certainly this goes on all the time. Read the newspapers. Look into your own heart. Look only momentarily, in case what you see causes you trauma and then you need therapy.

No one has ever sickened of his will when it was properly rooted, but more of that later. There is first of all the world-will, and that is the one that overwhelms us or convicts us, even damns us, of an insufficiency that leaves us mortals struggling for excuses to exist. We have this inbuilt need for perception, and while we try to fill this need in terms of measurement and system, of things and all that we suppose pertains to them, we run aground – which is, by the way, the general direction we should have chosen in the first place. Mind you, choosing, and having our nose pushed into, those are not the same in the eyes of our vanity.

So is the desire to be perfect at the bottom of it all? In a sense, yes. In a sense we know ourselves to be wicked, to be quite imperfect, morally and ethically speaking. But we have a secret notion that we became that way, and that therefore we once were perfect – even though the usual perception of time does not ever quite seem to suffice for an illustration of that 'once upon a time'.

The world-will, in short, turns out time and again not to have been a very useful response to this deep-seated need for this perfection. It tantalizes, with promises of power, fame, pleasure and such like, but it does not finally produce the goods. What it does finally produce is despair, sickness and madness, and no one in his right mind can wax very enthusiastic about these. It leads, among other things, to a notion of good and evil, a kind of ideal and idealistic good and evil, that bears the stamp of bitter disappointment, both in advance and in hindsight. We cannot for long do without some notion of good and evil, this is true, but the one that arises out of world-will, or conversely out of our unavoidable disenchantment with it, is not worth a second look, because whatever it accomplishes, it will not help us towards the real perfection and wholeness we need and crave.

Finally, then, we turn away from 'all these things', or so we suppose, and we curse them, or we regard them with a studied indifference, or we try to amuse ourselves at their expense, all in the interest of something we might be tempted to call suffering. "I cannot, I cannot get to the mountain!" we cry out, or sigh in defeat. "Let the mountain come to me." So we sit tight and dig in our heels and what we need to hold out, in addition to self-consolation and self-justification, in addition to irony, mockery, sarcasm and a million other devices, is, after all, nothing other than the fuel and motivation to keep these going, which is our old friend the will to world and its representations. The man who had made a slave of his spouse became so bored that he 'decided' to let her tyrannize him instead. Hopeless in either case, but he ended up with what he strangely enough chose to call the will to suffer. What does he promise himself? Why this about-face?

He simply came to the end of a road. The explanation seems to lie ready at hand, at least to him. He is so sick and tired of seeing his best efforts frustrated, for no reasons that make any sense to him, that he ceases from effort. But of course the world right away piles in on him, with all the old promises and seductions, so he has to make an effort to cease from making an effort. The world-will, after all is not free, but everywhere physiologically determined and psychologically formed, or deformed.

We will not get rid of this world-will by turning our back on it, whether we do it reluctantly or resolutely. The inborn urge to be whole, to be hale and hearty and merry to boot, nags away at us like a spouse who has our best interests at heart but cannot quite make herself understood, so she employs spurious devices – and we despise her for it. We would do better to examine our reactions to her.

*

The only way to be rid of the world-will, of the will that defines itself in terms of the world and the world in its own image, offensive as that sounds, is to come up with another will altogether. No use trying to alter the world-will, to squeeze it into a different pattern or to offer it different jobs to do. No, quite a different and new will has to be invented and brought out into the open, a will that is happy to leave the world as it is, to give it the benefit of every doubt possible.

Our hopes rise when we hear of such a will and willingness. Our hopes, shall we say, rise again. For we had lost hope. Now we hear that a will is possible quite distinct from the world and its tortures and allurements. Why, that would once again bring us within scope and handhold of the sound mind and body we so persistently crave. Are we then after all to bestride the earth, not like demons or invalids, but as happy human beings?

It comes to us in a way that we could not expect or anticipate, this hope for a new and world-distinct will, and it is true that we must be ready for the unexpected even while we hope for that which cannot be anticipated. Quite remarkably our urge, that urge for perfection, has become a hope for it. There is a world of difference between an urge and hope. Urgency comes upon us and we do not always right away take kindly to it. It would dictate terms to us, while we prefer to pick and choose. But now, after disappointed will and the 'will to suffer', we have decided to hope for perfection, for being able to exist in the round and under no restraints except those that further life and perhaps even a certain liveliness.

The worldly will is in the throes of being replaced by the hopeful will. We gladly confess ourselves as one of the number who are undergoing this change. It may take some time, but we are in for it for however long it takes. Hope until now has seemed to us a rather silly pastime. And so it would have been, while harnessed to our will for and of world. Now it turns in our hands into an incredibly and unpredictably effective instrument, into a powerful tool for change.

Are we seriously suggesting that a hope for being whole can lead to whole being? It does not so much lead to it as it is just that. It is the hope that is linked directly and immediately into that urgency, that urge for perfection, for perfect being and for being perfect. The urge becomes hope. We hear of it, of the fact that this is possible, and we see a few actual examples of it in practice, and then, gradually, we begin to move in that direction ourselves. If, at first, our hope is, from sheer bad habit, tied into this or that silly attainment, this causes us no great consternation, for we discern from the start that the hoping is the thing, and not this or that habitually silly attainment, which we neither fight nor confirm.

The organic nature of this urgently hopeful will is that it forever runs over into works. It seems I cannot successful hope for myself alone. My health must be able to spill over into yours. If you are not well, you who at this moment are close to me, then my hope automatically springs fresh for our sake and on our behalf, and my own perfection, momentarily sidetracked, rises to new heights and widens to fresh distances. This may be a novel way of speaking about perfection, as something that involves rank and degree, but it seems novel to us only because we have in the past limited ourselves to the perfection of things, mistaking even ourselves and one another for things. Who has not thought of the final salvation as something beyond which no living can reach!

Now it occurs to me at last how my own hope to be whole is the same as yours. On this level and within this context of our urgent hope our whole being in unison emerges.

However, how is it you behave when I show you this perfection and when I express this hope, not really being able to do other than show and express? How do you feel in the presence of this organic hope? Do you right away joyfully shout: "Yes, this is what I want, what I need, let me be part of it!"? If not, then why not? Is it perhaps with you now as it was with me when my world-will was challenged by a hopeful willing? Can it be otherwise than that in the presence of a greater perfection? We at first become painfully aware of our lesser perfection, and we resist this greater perfection, strive against it and strike out at it.

So evidently there is once again a need for suffering, though this is a suffering of another kind altogether. While the greater perfection approaches and I feel within me the resistance rising, then this is the time for suffering on my part, so that this greater perfection may be mine. To the degree that I resist and refuse to suffer I shall be in pain. Then, if I suffer this perfection to come unto me and as I grow in it, stronger in hope and wholeness, and then I approach you with it, and you resist, reject and revile, do I help you, or myself, by hating you for this, and by in turn reviling you now? No doubt initially I will be surprised, taken aback. Perhaps I was far too full of myself and needed a health-giving antidote. (The fact that you intended no such thing does not prevent it from working like that.) But then, hopefully, I can see that once again this is a time for suffering on my part. You want to punish me for causing, in you, this consciousness of a lesser perfection, of a comparative imperfection and I can choose not to hold this against you, not to pay you back in kind, but instead to hope for your sake, on your behalf, so that you may find your way out of this world-wilfulness into a wholeness of hopeful willing. Then, perhaps, next time you will do the same for me, when I am stuck in some apparently insufferable condition and willing only to see my right and my painful self.

So we can see now how the hopeful will to suffer is something quite different from the worldly will to suffer. In the case of the latter we are disappointed by our failure to will successfully as we see fit and so we throw ourselves into painful situations and insist, as it were, on damage and destruction, our own as much as everyone else's, if we but realized it. In the case of the former, we understand the nature of growth to greater perfection and our suffering is conscious behaviour, at once remedial and introductory. Indeed this hopeful willing which we have identified here for the sake of understanding, in comparison to worldly willing, is always at one and the same time a suffering, and where a discrepancy sets in between willing and suffering, so that we do first one then the other, we are caught up in pain again and in a worldly will, and we need help.

(27/12/'95)

7

Human Distinction

One of our worst fears is to be of no use. We equate this with being worthless. We imagine that to be born must mean to be

43

born to some end, though we do not always insist that we should be able to recognize that end. We are sometimes satisfied with a vague notion of it, because we manage to make ourselves believe that if we took more pains we could readily find out.

A distinct human being is one who needs no further assurance of his reason for being around, not because he is too unconscious to care but because he has worked out his destiny to a degree where his being and his working have begun to merge into one. He is and he does at one and the same time. We observe him from a distance and feel justified in calling him a truly fortunate man.

And yet close up he does not necessarily inspire our confidence. Our minds are accustomed to the contemplation of idols, sad to say, and idols do not live. They are not in human contact with other beings. In fact they themselves are not beings but things, and we have elevated them to a level of admiration because they cannot harm us by reminding us of our shortcomings. An idol always remains safely remote, especially while we flatter its powerful endowments. We have made the thing ourselves and now we behave as though it existed in its own right.

A distinct human being cannot help but remind us that we ourselves are less than distinct – or indistinct. He makes no effort to do this; it happens automatically. Here is a person who is no longer anxious abut the way he fits into the scheme of things: he exists in relation to the truth and he knows it. His outward aspect is one over which he exercises no amount of control. We in comparison still suppose we must manipulate appearances in order to achieve a desired effect. Our traditional delusions are not shared by him, hence we are prone to accuse him of irreverence. When we inquire into his fundamental beliefs he informs us he has none. This disconcerts us.

No doubt we all have a longing for distinction. We address our fondest hopes to a being that should single us out for special attention. We aggravate ourselves in the interest of some high attainment so that others might point to us, or point us out for emulation. Not that we necessarily wish to benefit anyone. It would do us if we were told by a sufficiently large number of people that our presence is appreciated – for whatever reason.

For the genuinely distinct human being this is not enough. He may be tempted to pay heed, but at bottom he knows that the consensus of a crowd does not signify. What he looks for is something that is akin to an inward certainty instinctively persuasive. Even his most poignant onsets of self-doubt must be overruled by something he does not need to conjure up by precarious means before it serves him. He knows he can go out on a limb and suddenly find himself on another tree. The constitution of his nerves is such that anxieties are bridges towards confidence, that high spirits are accidents with an as yet undiscovered purpose.

His attitude towards death is worth looking at. How a man views the cessation of his conscious ego, and whether he bothers, or dares, to view it at all, this characterizes him for us, especially if we ourselves entertain certain high-frequency affect-complexes in connection with the topic. We may not frequently make death a topic of discussion, but it seems difficult to live if we know nothing of death, just as it must prove problematic to do good if we know nothing of evil. And a great mass of cancelled opinions does not make for very lively brain processes. Indeed the opposite is the case. Which encourages us in our ambition to tackle now what might be called the distinct human being's application to his brain, and his use, or even enjoyment, of something called brain-power.

This comes along with distinction of the sort we mean here, and we can safely insist that the distinct human being is the only one who is not mastered by his brain but instead is aware of it as an available organic function of a very specific nature. Lesser human beings (and I apply the concept of rank advisedly) would literally be shocked out of their minds if they were suddenly, without prior preparation in the realm of creativity, given a lively experience of what voluntarily solicited brain power amounts to. Indeed he would be astonished to the point of incredulity if he were informed truthfully and correctly of the degree of mental effort and bodily agitation that he expends and tolerates so as to avoid the practical consequences of such a solicitation. What exactly is he worried about? We have to tread carefully here. A single step in the wrong direction can cause a setback with painful consequences. The problem might be defined in the following manner. Access to the riches of the brain is exclusively for those with clean hands who are able to hold out for an indefinite period of time under the constellation of self-analysis without moving a single finger in that direction. Happily certain safeguards are built into the average human constitution that disallow premature 'cerebration', as we might call it for the moment. These safeguards are very rarely correctly understood, and indeed this is not important, since what matters is that they work, not that we know that they exist or how they come to be in existence, as apparent curses that are actually blessings, in the first place. Enough said that we must be somewhat coaxed and wooed, by both circumstances and individual inclination, into the correct position from where the crucial advent of a brain impulse, or pulse, may be responsibly entertained. The accent is of course on response, on our own ability to respond, and beyond that on our willingness to respond ethically. A brain pulse into an ignorant and stupid constitution is a stroke of lightning, and we even refer to someone under such circumstances as suffering a stroke. Temporary or permanent paralysis sets in and of course the same thing is liable to occur again.

On the other side of the spectrum we can describe the well prepared, or fortunate constitution, where, for example, a true willingness exists to do good and to be human. The willingness to do good and to have a beneficial effect on those around us, however clumsily one actually manages, works like a yeast in our entire system, so that it would not be an exaggeration to say that he who is willing to do good is differently constituted – on account of that willingness.

As for being human, this must attract us not so much as a novelty but as an overriding concern, an habitual care that in turns nags at us and motivates us for years before we are even in an inward position – or of a fitting disposition – to identify it correctly and behave in line with it, aware of what we do. We are not born with this willingness to be human rather than popular. What we are born with is a great mixture of conflicting affects and moods, plus, of course, the developing ability, alas, to weigh and to choose. And humanity does at times appear as a choice among many and not frequently are we persuaded by the necessity to choose this one boon or perish. The prevailing culture of our environment as we grow up shows perhaps no trace of a distinction between humanity and popularity, between human beings and people, so that the road is hard for us and the opportunities for error, even fatal error, manifold.

*

It is the desire to do good and to be human that prepares us suitably and sufficiently for the advent of brain power, so that when the time is ripe we no longer run away from our brain but we are able to access it. An energetic individual may suppose that he uses his brain but in fact what he does is react fearfully to what he envisions as an accident, or the possibility of an accident 'up there'. If we look forward to a marriage of heart and head, so that will and intellect, emotion and reason, work hand in hand, we equally anticipate a unity of brain and brawn. Brain on its own is really a computer, nothing more, and one can get on splendidly without it. A developed 'mere' brain causes mischief and creates monsters – though not the brain, but we ourselves are at fault. As for brawn on its own – well, we have horses for that, and mechanical horsepower. The popular inventions of man are born out of the fear of human distinction. Strangely we are afraid of nothing so much as of becoming the way we were, of returning to the shape in which we were created. The marvels of our civilization become irrelevant as soon as human beings turn out the way they were conceived. What we leave behind on our way to human distinction could be said to be very small in comparison to what we gain – if, indeed, a common denominator existed. The fact that it does not, accentuates the importance of ethical action as the bridge from one to the other. An indistinct human being is miserable, unhappy and sick. He cannot function in his own right and therefore experiences the world as a realm of relative injustice. He compares himself to people and is bound to draw the most unfortunate conclusions. People are scandalized by the comparison, so they shun him, suppress him and lock him up, if they do not flatter him, bribe him and then destroy him. Indistinct human beings make people nervous, because people know that no such thing as humanity really exists, while indistinct human beings forever challenge that knowledge. Nothing more absurd than a human being challenging popular knowledge. Nothing more tragic than a human being succumbing to popular knowledge. People know what they know and their justification lies in their numbers.

Of course an indistinct human being must be plagued by people, else how will he come round to reversing his direction? Unless of course he caves in. This indistinction is not merely a lack of distinction or a case of 'distinction not yet' but a horrible misunderstanding, something like a cruel joke of fate, because a one who should, according to all the rules and regulations of a sound physical constitution, ally himself to his own kind and learn the tricks of his trade – namely original creativity, authentic responsibility, uniquely individual personality – has instead forsaken his own kind and looks to people for his community, for his audience and reward. How passionately he tries to refashion himself, in the eyes of these unappreciative ones, who can

48

recognize only what is exuded by their pores, so that reality remains for them the shadow of a spectre! Alas he is never on such dangerous ground as when he pleases them. Bad enough if he should accidentally please them – but as an ambition?

The indistinct one ends by apologizing for his own foot prints – or by committing the original crime. Established religions would have him burdened with original sin, and to please those masters of indistinction he is willing to rise to the occasion. We lose interest in him, he has nothing left to lose because he has nothing, not because he has it all.

The distinct one has it all, and no one can take it from him. Even his response to gravity is fraught with value. The elements entice him and he entices them back. What he makes of himself today he squanders tomorrow, a firm believer in the fact that nothing human is wasted. Does he need to apply himself to justify his existence? Not at all, for he knows that he is, which knowledge more than suffices. His activities are celebrations of his existence and he proudly puts himself on show. He is distinguished by life. Life itself points to him and smiles approval. As he lives he knows that he equally lives for his indistinct brothers, who hopefully may be moved to imitation by his example. Of sacrifice he knows nothing. Never does he wish to be thanked for helping. Most of all he would prefer to remain anonymous in this department. He longs for peers, for brothers, not for dependants or fans. When the time comes for him to close his eyes he welcomes the dark and acknowledges the silence as a blessing. Are the perhaps his own children? Has he not raised them to the light? To articulate speech? To dance and music?

Suddenly he can no longer imagine an end to his existence, and then he knows that he has 'survived'. He has come to the end of every possible end and he blesses the world. What he becomes now for those who have seen him is a new vision, for those who have touched him a new heart. And for those who have wished him well he becomes for all time a quickening inspiration, and the greatest possible help to distinction.

———

(1/1/'96)

8

Life as the Dance

We are not to be imitated, examples of life that we are, and each one of us persuasive to his end in his own way. Do we know of one another? Is it important that we should?

A wreath on the grave of these last two millennia is our sincerest contribution to their recorded state. Do we hate anything worse than having to explain ourselves? Than having to justify our behaviour?

Our favourite occupation amounts to nothing more – and to nothing less – than a repetition of ourselves for others. Who these others are is more their concern than ours. Our works make us known to those who would know us, that much suffices, while any efforts to change the world or its motley inhabitants would lay upon us the unreasonable burden of a tax on our credibility.

Are we not made to celebrate, even in our senses, the sheer luxury of humanity as spirit and flesh? Should we not sit and reflect for a fortnight, our chin on our fist, on the moribund state of the earth's population and then give it the most effective push imaginable in the direction of freedom by finding – our reflections expressly delightful?

We who raise no more objections to humanity because we know it in its essence and greet it in one another, why are we not much more sought out and honoured? Are we perhaps not yet ready to be set on a pedestal and ignored.

Time and space do not limit our effectiveness. The ease with which we flit from fact to deed to prayer and satisfaction would make the wren envious, or a breeze through the orchard. We are light-footed on the basis of spontaneity and we are not afraid to call it a compulsion, if need be, to get the better of it, but in any case to continue.

We have cracked the universal nut of pain and we eat the kernel called sensible suffering. There is nothing to be learned from us that cannot be learned as readily from a tiger in the wild, from a cherry blossom bough or from the sunshine of a summer's day. Like these we too have our seasons, our precarious appearances to the uninformed eye. Like these we arouse the fruitful imagination and urge it to its task of a lively development.

Really our strength is bottomless since our weakness gives birth to it. A single leap as an archway from certainty to doubt illustrates all possible connections that make for universal variety and splendour. Our hearts are endowed with a thousand eyes and we never feel the urge to draw the sum of their perspectives. Nothing is finite except insofar as we embrace it in gratitude and shower it with generosity, which we do with a vengeance, since finite things, their eternal coming and going, are for us a feast and the earnest of a glad resurrection. Really we like to hold out under the onslaught of misfortune and we know of nothing better to do, since misery brings us the skill of mercy and despair amounts to our tributary into an all-complete joy. How can we possibly be disappointed, since disappointment itself announces its meaning as a signal of success? We would like to be honoured not for our achievements but for the simple reality of our personhood.

*

Looking into the eyes of a perfect human being opens vistas of personal experience. Certainly no one would think of stopping to examine the source of that effect. If it suddenly seems worthwhile to breathe the air of our worn-out environment, why would we question the cause of that benefit? No, we breathe lustily and make plans again for our future. A delicious commotion has influenced our limbs, our organs are in the market for novelty. All our opinions and ideas are swept away as so much poor property that fits into no house. We have seen into the soul of a whole person. Our capacity for affection has come to our notice, we are impressed with it and we search the horizon for an object worthy of absorbing it and thriving. Even then do those objects turn into beings, discovering their true nature to us, for we held them in disrespect, unloading upon their appearances habitually the prejudices of our resentful mind, the presumptions of our cowardly heart. It happens to us now, with a persuasive vitality, what we previously stalked and chased across the parched reaches of our indifferent sensibilities. We are anointed. We have what it takes to make of ourselves a child of good fortune. We have hobnobbed with royalty and shall never return to the hovel of our envious inclinations, of our indolent tendencies. The one in whose presence we tasted our inborn sanctity has long passed away and left us with an appetite for excellence and with an abhorrence for the treachery which we knew then only as our rights. We forgive all evil as an imbalance of style.

*

And so, too, we forgive the temporal life. The implications of this life, the natural red in tooth and claw aspect for example, and along with that, of course, all efforts to prolong, enhance or subdue it, do not any more fascinate us, neither do they make us blanch. It bears for us the aspect of the expected, of the "what can you expect under the circumstances". The murderer has lashed out and we know what he means. We count his regeneration as crucial as that of the socially innocent. For does not society breed its own vices, by dint of being Society? How often does this temporal life not once again stand in need of being underscored as the provisional thing it is, irrespective of cultures and civilizations. The two-edged reminder might as well be interpreted as providential. There is no need to wait for the enfeebled state of 'fight for survival', for the self-made victim and slave. Equally the tyrant, equally the arbitrary puppet of fate, all carnage in his wake, may be viewed all the more realistically with the merciful eye; it sees him more clearly.

This merciful attitude towards the temporal life facilitates our perseverance – in ourselves; I would say: in what we hold most dear. Who, nowadays, when virtually all the cards are on the table and the most esoteric rumours are headlines, would still wish to be implicated in this life, even by the merest rejection of it! No, the eternal life lovingly swallows the temporal up. Some still desire to take sides – as they forfeit their perspective.

*

The pall of 'the nothing' settles on the dancer and leaves him – nonplussed. Sure, he must have his vacation. What, no vacuum in the universe? He knows better, from experience. That suddenly all space should collapse, just when he has it all measured out with his movements, is really no surprise to him. If it does somewhat take him aback, he seeks the reason for this in nothing more than a moment's inattention. If time disappears just after he has touched it he rushes into the breach and blesses its absence. He himself would rather for the predictable interval share in the fate of the puppet than argue with fate and cause lethargy to slip into his limbs due to an entertained annoyance. Why not be a puppet for now! he decrees, as he winks at the one with the strings in his hand, who has become more tangible since all else has faded. Why not hang for a spell in the blinding consciousness of creation? Why not lie in a heap on the boards, weighed down by nothing but a few wires? Soon the skin will begin to itch, giving the lie to the wood. A tug, and the new figure stands, quivering with the readiness to demonstrate constant change.

*

We who have danced our way into the heart of the human perspective do not mind being mistaken, by those still innocent of change, for their own kind, temporarily. It does no harm.

53

Total inertia is, in a sense, like perfect movement. We may speak of the grace of insouciant convention, even while at a loss for an explanation of it. There are those who accuse us of attending enthusiastic inspiration before we dance, and their error concerns us a little more. It seems their blame is shrouded in flattery. They reward us for being what we decidedly are not. But our care is for those who would join us in the dance and we would not have them misled. Woe to those who insist on being moved before they move. These incessant dreamers, who themselves stay out of harm's way due to an accidental constitution, how should we manage to get them to espouse responsibility? Their flourishes excite, their sighs depress, and gravity is never, never once, celebrated. We concrete dancers know gravity almost as our spouse. Far from perverting our sexuality, she establishes our gender. We are 'married' to the weight of our flesh, and we hate it when that impulse to kick loose overcomes us. We do not dance to feel weightless, or to help others feel weightless, but to festively carry our weight. The woods are full of the moral – and not only moral – arbitrators between the bad carnal and the good spiritual. We cannot with the best of wills see it like that. Spirit and flesh are one, not just joined at the hip for the duration. No contract needs to be forged, to safeguard an idle pretence. Spirit is one way of looking at it and flesh is the other. And what is 'it'? Spirit or flesh. This must be danced. It cannot be argued, with a will of lording it over an opposite opinion. It gathers no comfort from any decision on the difference between right and wrong. All that is real is one, and of infinite variety. Where divorce is supposed, the root of it lies in the not yet perceptive organ of perception. Those who still need to be healed shall not dictate the parameters of health. At best they can come up with an ideal health, and we cannot prevent them from clinging, as to crutches, to their healthy ideals. Meanwhile, for ourselves, we are bound, as a consequence, to dance all those ideals away.

We have got the message, and we shall not now settle down with the messenger; good grief! perhaps even at his feet? Rather let us do combat now and again, if need be, with the delusion of the bottomless pit; at least that is honest work. We dance out into 'pure' space and no one can say what supports us. Because no one can say, does that mean what nothing is there? Our dancing is control of the fact that the truth of the matter resides elsewhere. Matter is resistance, but where the resistance is sublimated matter does not cease to exist, it merely becomes impossible to follow, which circumstance, when all is said and done, should annoy no one but the materialist. He cannot help but experience our dancing at this stage very much as a curse, though we would like to help him out. The delusion of mere space, of empty space, divorced from time and its material illustration, has its moral equivalent, and what springs to mind is the modern lie, which dictates that men, women and children can be good. This dictatorship, especially when disguised as a religion, really does pull the rug out – and the floor too – from beneath the feet of those who feel inwardly urged to dance. Before they even begin to learn, their first faltering steps are criticized. 'This is not good', they are told, 'you should throttle those urges. Be good and behave in the time-honoured fashion like those who approve of you. Let nothing be new under the sun.

Ah, but the sun is new, and this above all else we would gloriously dance. There is a new sun in a new sky. The elements are no longer at war. A flame flickers in a beam of light, a breeze plays over a lump of clay, while a stream cleanses and slakes. We are part of this and it looks to our benevolent concession. Then it becomes part of us.

Finally excellence makes no demands on those who flirt with knowledge and bear her no children. Our most extraordinary emissary comes from the clouds, is cloud, and reveals himself in a whirl of dance. Have faith now in the sagacity of

your incandescent soul while your limbs fly and flash, in tune
with the earth's biological fervour. So much that creeps into
our existence like a sluggish inhibition transforms the day upon
our cheerful acceptance of it, as disguised energy, in tribute to
our human celebration as dancers.

(2/1/'96)

9

For Arthur

What exactly do you mean? Is it wrong to be happy?
Shouldn't we look forward to feeling good?

*

A: That's it. Looking forward to feeling good is a waste of
time. The mature person takes 'feeling good' and 'feeling bad'
as equal quantities.

B: I find that irritating, this talk of 'the mature person'.

A: Alright then, look at the pain you have, the depression,
the anxiety, the stomach ache, and for heaven's sake know
once and for all that these are growing pains, all of them, and
that they can be eased by you, but only in a creative manner, if
you acknowledge every time that they are signs of some benefit
coming your way, and if you let your primary interest and mental content be not the removal of the pain but the acceptance of
that as yet unknown benefit.

B: It sounds too complicated. Do you want me to turn into a
masochist? Should I cause myself pain?

A: You do that right now, by taking an interest in your
pains, and that is unfortunate. You should forbid yourself entirely to talk about what hurts you for at least six months, and
every time you want to start again, practice instead this gentle
recognition of the Christ as the resurrection, as the one who is
born out of pain and bears out of pain. I believe we know each
other well enough for me to be able to tell you that whenever

you merely take note and stock of your ailments, turning them this way and that way, describing them, complaining about them or acting as if they did not exist – you actually betray the very source of all health and happiness because you do not instead kindly solicit the aid of the one who is present at that very moment in you as merciful love. You see, if he were not moving in you, you would not be agitated or depressed.

B: You mean he causes my pain?

A: On the contrary. You are the cause of your own pain because you have not yet, in that particular instance, turned to him and to his reality, which can of course only be done in faith and not with the senses.

B: Why is this so difficult to understand?

A: Because we spend so much time 'understanding' the opposite. We are never done 'understanding' the various causes of our weakness, of our insanities and illnesses, as if there were profit in that. The good lies in understanding the good, standing under it, like a tree under the sun and the rain. But in order to achieve this good understanding we have to, for Christ's sake, quieten our intellect and discipline our feelings. I find it disgusting, how often I myself indulge in brain-wracking …

B: You mean brain-racking, don't you?

A: Both, come to think of it, because it 'wracks' the brain – anyway, I indulge in that, and in the dissection of my feelings; and this happens like an accident, I certainly do not decide to do it but suddenly find myself doing it …

B: Why not simply turn away from it?

A: It's so fascinating! I find myself so fascinating when I'm wallowing once again in …

B: Shouldn't I be saying this?

A: I have given myself the commandment, that I will frequently ask myself how I am, and if I 'feel good' then I am going to be on my guard, and if I feel poorly somewhere, in mind, body, soul, flesh or spirit, then I am going to call to mind what

I know regarding the significance of pain, namely that it signals a fortunate change, a change in reality in my favour, and then I am going to make it my chief occupation actually to be cheerful and glad about this –

B: How can you voluntarily feel cheerful and glad? That is absurd. You would be working yourself up into a falsehood!

A: Quite right. But I said I would <u>be</u> cheerful and glad, not <u>feel</u> it. Why must you always confuse those two? Your faith is the motivator of your being. You can be precisely as you wish, if you wish faithfully. You can <u>be</u> glad while you <u>feel</u> miserable. In fact I suggest that you do that. Every time you feel miserable, be glad.

B: You want me to be glad that I am miserable?

A: Good heavens, what is it with you? Have you a one-track mind?

B: Just explain and stop hectoring.

A: Of course I don't want you to be glad that you are miserable. I want you to be glad because, as your misery shows, you have once again been gifted by your maker. The only difference between being glad that it's Christmas and being glad when a misery has arrived is that you associate pleasant sensations with Christmas itself, while in the case of the misery you associate a marvellous reality, revealing itself gradually, the way a loaf rises, as integrity, strength of character, childlike joy, beneficial personality, wise insight and all sorts of creative abilities that assure you of your communal usefulness.

B: Do tell.

A: So the way to all these real benefits is through a cheerful acceptance of our miserable individuality, and we are totally at liberty to lean on the one who has set us the efficient example, and this means following him. Do you feel helpless? Be glad and be one with the one who stuck it out to the end when he was totally helpless. Do you feel like lording it over others because you are a Christian? Shame on you.

B: Do you not like Christians?

A: You see, it's a matter of persevering, in a confident, quiet and intimate kind of a way. There are no group solutions to anything that I can see. Everybody has to work out his own peculiar relationship to his creator, like every son to his father. Our work depends on that. Everybody ends up making his own sort of contribution to the commonweal of humanity, and in the department of works no one can dictate for anyone else. I am not down on Christians but lukewarm time-servers disgust me. They are inwardly closed to the creative spirit and outwardly they make a show of blessedness. Give me the man with the troubled conscience, with the leaning to depression and high spirits. Give me the man who is plagued by aches and pains, by sinful thoughts and suicidal tendencies. But then let him take pains to learn of the significance and meaning of pain; let him understand pain as something for which there is a good reason, and let him then concentrate on that good reason. If he believes in god, then let him also abide with the one who comes from god and is with him now, who wants to be used, not just talked about.

B: There is so much talk, so much sheer language about and around the Christ, so much jargon, and so little actual trust.

A: Then work on that. Trust more. If you can see the fault, the remedy must be in you. I quite agree, by the way. Every time we complain about our lot we abuse trust. I frequently complain. But then I am ashamed of myself and make up for it like that. Of what should I complain? Of the fact that I am a human being who is being urged back to that state of perfection in which the human being was originally conceived?

B: But all that Christian jargon – is it not just an attempt to lie oneself back into that halfway house in which the modern psyche has languished for two-thousand years?

A: Could be. I don't know. If you do feel strongly about that, then maybe just there you should make your contribution. Avoid all jargon. Pretend you are not a Christian but follow Jesus all the more effectively. – Maybe this conversation should end.

B: I am going to add up my real experiences and see what comes out in the end.

A: Count your abilities instead, your spiritual faculties, and put them into harness. Every writer who becomes a disciple of the kingdom of heaven is like a householder who brings out of his storeroom things both new and old. Mathew thirteen, I believe. – Are we not rewarded according to our behaviour?

B: I have so much energy at times. On occasion I feel desperately weak. I swing from self-congratulation to self-flagellation, from killing others with kindness to abusing them with my alleged superior wisdom.

A: Join the club.

B: You mean at your age you are still not free of that?

A: Why should I be free of it? Do you want me to be dead? What I am pretty well free of is the wish to be free of all that. Every day brings along with it, for me personally, a finite number of problems, of pains, of sheer inconveniences, and these are my raw materials, my signposts, my handholds on the work of the spirit. If I were you I should insist on being cured for all time of the desire to be finished with god.

B: But then that would be just another mistake, would it not?

A: Of course. Tell me then how you might handle that desire.

B: I would welcome it like an old friend and say to it: You want me to be finished with god? You want me to be a shining halo around the curly locks of an angel? You want me to be able to stretch back on my hammock and let the sun shine up my nostrils with never a care in the world, so that I can gloat, and pity the unfortunates of the word? Is that what you want?

A: That's not bad at all for a start. That should take the wind out of its sail for that time. And it's a very lively description of

60

something too. I love to see trust in action. Deep down everyone does. It's so unassuming, so unpretentious.

B: Perhaps for you. For me trust can fling itself about a bit.
I am young and I adhere to the convictions of my youth. I even
call them beliefs. I need to experiment with sanity a bit, and
with my natural functions.

A: Look, over there; those two women, trying to get on that
bus at the same time. They'll not make it, they're stuck. Amaz-
ing! There, one of them is going to have to go first. The driver
is laughing.

10

The Collective Will

This is something worth looking at, not, mind you, so as to
learn something from it but so as to be rid of it again, for the
sake of a communal voice instead. Many things need to be
looked, even though it horrifies us to stare in that direction because we fear we may not be able to avert our gaze in time. The
sheer fascination can be overwhelming.

Some avoid crowds for no other reason. Others study something called crowd psychology, or group sociology, or they
speak of the will of the masses. We do well to be careful. The
extinct sciences, unintentionally or at least unconsciously, kill
off the thing they so rigorously pursue. The live sciences pursue other things, and for quite different reasons. Our desire to
understand must literally be informed by a conscientious wish
to gain sensible access to infinite knowledge, for the purpose of
understanding. That infinite knowledge should arrive at finite
and practical conclusions – no extinct scientist can come to
terms with that; except, of course, by becoming other than he is.

Now what we mean by the collective will here is certainly
infinite in nature, there is no arguing with that. I am apt to have

an onset of it at any time, and so are you. This proves nothing except that I have something to gain by overcoming it. It does not point to any badness in me that allows for this will. My human condition is such, by definition, that I am open to all manner of influence, and so also to the collective will. I would not wish it to be otherwise. What separates the men from the boys is the standpoint that is taken in the presence of this will. In the face of it we have the choice to become popular or more human. A rather fundamental choice, you might say, and you would be right.

So we need to identify the thing we mean here. On the surface of it it feels good, it feels nice, it seems pleasant and often downright flattering, even right at the start. And the influence of it can start any time; it may even startle. Of course it makes all the difference in the world how we are, and perhaps who we are, at the moment of the influence. Sometimes we are thrown, bowled over by it, and then we wallow in the warm bath of it for some time before our eyes are opened and perception is possible again. We may even instigate an occasion of it, such as after a bout of loneliness, a period of accidental isolation from others. There are those who consider themselves properly alive only while under the influence of this energy, and in the absence of it they suppose they die. They need to be persuaded that on he contrary, only in the absence of it can real life take hold and accumulate, and that the presence of it is a sham. Mere words will not succeed. They will have to be shown, by active and careful example. This short essay is such an example.

This collective will, then, is an energy that superficially pleases but in reality it destroys what can be destroyed. If we have life in us, this cannot be destroyed, so this energy cannot make inroads there. But if we have no real life in us, we may well be devastated. This energy is vast. It takes with one hand what it gives with the other. And it seduces us not while we are by ourselves in the quietness of our own room but while we are among others, whatever our reason for being among them.

We can, by the way, seek out the company of others for the purpose of overcoming this will, but then we have to know very well what we do; we have to be fully in the possession of ourselves. This is worthwhile in any case, but of especial importance if ever we should decide to subject ourselves to its influence for the purpose of overcoming it. And remember that its presence may occur to us in a great variety of ways so that we should never feel complacent, supposing we have 'finally solved the problem'. After all, should the time ever come that we do have it under control for our own individuality, then we may tackle occurrences of it in others inasmuch as we allow these to affect us, compassionately. A total absence of the collective will is not to be contemplated. Our own individuality, the way we are under given circumstances independently from others, is always open at least to the illusion of impersonal society, by which I mean the quite wrong supposition that we can agree with one another or have intercourse of a lasting nature without having to overcome what we dislike and hate about one another. All attempts at impersonal society are doomed from the outset because a fundamental aspect of human nature is not taken into consideration, namely our *desire to triumph*, by which I mean an appetite for being the best. This appetite exists in us from birth and it can be perfectly satisfied, though this happens rarely, as history testifies. What happens most commonly is that judgment according to appearances interferes with it. What we get then is failure upon failure, and each seems like a success. A residual appetite is then developed for these seeing successes, and for an accumulation of them, in the misguided hope that a sufficient number of shams will eventually amount to the genuine article.

But what, precisely, is this triumph towards which we strive, intelligently or in ignorance? Can we imagine it, first of all?

The fact of the matter is, we can not. It can only make sense to each one of us in terms of our own eventual achievement, and what we enjoy as foretastes of it is to egg us on, to encourage and stimulate us, and finally even to punish us, in the true sense of the word 'punishment', which implies a forcible correction.

If we cannot imagine it, then how are we to proceed? We experience the appetite but we cannot imagine what will satisfy it. What is more, to each of us this appetite occurs in such a fashion that we cannot satisfactorily explain or describe it to anyone else, so that in the end, after numerous attempts, we are thrown back again on this appetite itself, in ourselves, while any relation of it to other experiences of it necessarily end up by occurring to us as futile. Such experiences are perhaps in turn experienced by us as defeats, where they might always be interpreted as pointers in the right direction.

We cannot climb out of our own individuality unaided. And of course there is no need to escape from it, though it may seems so to us, and very painful. We come to the pass where everything to do with our individuality becomes hateful to us and we simply want rid of it. Suicide is such a reflex. The notion that we should escape from that which makes us different from everyone else, or that we should destroy it, is the result of ultimate disappointment, and it can be seen as the other side of the coin, as when we insist on being individuals and individualists.

So we know that we cannot escape from our individuality and that we cannot remain with our individuality. The collective will brings this painfully home to us, which is like a negative perception of the truth of the matter. The truth is that we want our individuality to grow into personality. A person is happy in the possession of his individuality, not coerced by it or inhibited by it. A person is glad to be different and unique.

The collective will, we can see now, at once painfully emphasizes our lack of personality and holds out the promise of an ideal individuality. A potential human being among people is affected like that. He realizes he does not fit in and instead of being glad, under the circumstances, he supposes that this points to some shortcoming in himself – which it does, of course, but not to the one he is told about by people, for they would like him as an ideal individual. His actual shortcoming however is insufficient or absent personality. The potential human being – every potential human being – is therefore for a time on a knife edge, tugged in the one direction by such pleasant promises or prestigious threats as these ideal individuals, as manufactured by the collective will, and pushed in the opposite direction by his human desire to triumph, to be perfect, which can also take the form of wishing to be finally happy and blessed.

Our desire to triumph as human beings must be personally addressed from without by a personal human being. There is no other way for us to find a handhold except that it is shown to us by another. People hold out to us, and up to us, the ideal individual, and this can drive us to distraction because we are not able to see through the lie which people use to dupe not only us, but first and foremost themselves. Even the very thing that is generally called society, this is based on the falsehood that impersonal individuality is not only possible, but desirable. The ideal, impersonal individual, the idealist, the individualist – these are endowed with charisma and even called personalities, though they have nothing of personality about them. A 'personality' is nothing more than an individualist who rides on public acclaim and popular esteem – for the simple reason that he is able to lie more persuasively. This falsehood has taken on monumental proportions.

Persons and personalities have absolutely nothing in common. The former have the collective will underfoot, while the latter serve the collective will and exist as illustrations of it.

*

We have altered our personality as soon as we have once again made of the collective will a thing of the past. Such alterations are to the good. Specifically, we might say, they sweeten our nature.

Overcoming this will means to triumph. This is triumph in truth and in reality. The triumph of the popular will, by comparison, is catastrophe and disaster. What matters for us is that we learn how to triumph and to more than triumph, by which latter expression I mean to indicate our excursions into the realm of the collective will for the purpose of works.

We know that we triumph when we wish to do so with all our strength. Indeed we may think of it as an exercise of strength even when we wish to triumph over the collective will. This wish motivates and moves our available human being and makes it manifest. It is the collective will to downgrade and annihilate human being. Therefore any manifestation of human being, in the light of day, gives strength immediately and directly to those who are still potentially human and robs those who serve the collective will of their voice even while they sense the breath of a new master.

Once we understand what it means to triumph in reality as human beings rather than supposedly as people, we may fasten this wish in our soul and there ally it to our spirit, so that both our spirit and soul may thenceforth, in unison, testify to truth and reality wherever we walk, which means we have power. The collective will to power has now come to nothing. An endless field of activity stretches out before us. The communal will has triumphed and continues to do so as we interpret as much of our experience as possible in the light of a preordained truthfulness to which we have access inwardly and which is then also revealed from without.

Once we have triumphed – and more than triumphed – the collective will no longer holds any terrors for us, mostly because we have learned how to overcome it, but also because we understand its counterproductive significance. This significance cannot occur to us in the light of day until we have managed largely to control our inhibitions and reactions, which implies a specifically ethical attitude towards people, an attitude which I would like to call eschatological. Mention of this near the end of this essay would seem appropriate.

It is an attitude which ensures firstly that we do not mistake human being for popularity, and secondly, that we take the fullest possible advantage of this counterproductivity that can come along with all of our experiences that are to any degree of a popular character. So, for example, there is the total lack of understanding for the truth which confronts us, so that we have the choice either to be disappointed, or else to confirm our standpoint so to speak on foreign territory, which is manageable if we overcome our disappointment by 'forgiving those who do not know what they do'. This forgiveness of popularity and of all things popular is crucial to the development of our human being. When people disappoint us, we do well to forgive them, because that gets us ahead. If we hold it against them, that holds us back.

I call this attitude of human forgiveness eschatological because it confronts and deals creatively every time with the last and final challenge of popularity to our human being. By 'last' I mean not one in an ascending series of stages, but the final stage leading to the end that lasts and is permanent. Then we have no more truck with the collective will in that particular department and we may go on to dedicate our new strength in service and by example to those who are still perplexed by their inability to triumph as they distinctly feel they should. Eventually they acquire even our attitude of forgiveness.

11

On Making a Fool of Oneself by Speaking as though one Knew.

And the thing is, one doesn't. It only comes over a person, this compulsion to speak, and then that person stops being a person, communicates no longer, expresses merely the collective will of those who are gathered, ostensibly, to communicate.

This collective will, then, is something one needs to anticipate. We need to know that it always lurks just around the corner. It looks for an opening, and then, like a bad smell, it pervades. Awareness is of the essence.

What is the collective will? Several have come together to get something done. Decisions are to be made. Problems are to be identified. Then comes the time for discussion. Suddenly the pressure is on everyone to make some useful contribution to the matter in hand. This pressure needs to be identified. Why is it so crucially important that this pressure be identified? Because it makes or breaks the sensible progress of the proceedings. It is as simple as this: While we are aware of this pressure, over any period of time, we make sense, which we can then articulate and communicate when the time is ripe. While we are not aware of this pressure it builds up some false image, both for ourselves and of ourselves, depending on whether we are just being subjective or objective, passive or active, lazy or excited. Whatever else we do, while this unidentified pressure is upon us we are constricted in falsehood, either within ourselves, morbidly, or outside ourselves, even beside ourselves, foolishly. The fool speaks without knowing what he says, he talks rubbish. He does not translate the communal pressure into sense but he dissipates it. He does not even know there is pressure. If he does feel it he only wants rid of it because he experiences every discomfort and every inconvenience by really not experiencing it at all but instead he slinks out of the way or else overleaps it as though it did not exist. He is an empty vessel, and we are all empty vessels under such 'collective circumstances', if the communal pressure is not identified so that one may be aware of it.

Awareness is the thing. Be aware of this pressure as though you were aware of a weight lying heavy on your shoulders, or of an enemy chasing you. Hold out under the weight and know that this translates it into sense. Turn around and face the enemy, and know that this makes sense. You want more sense, so that you can help make the decisions, identify the problems and advance the discussion. You would like as much sense as possible. Sense is made. It has to be made on the spot under such conditions as we describe here. And it does make sense to carry the weight and to face the enemy. How can we do that unless we first identify the pressure and the urgency?

It can also occur to us not as a pressure like weight but as an urgency. This urgency is what I mean by the enemy before whom we are likely to slink away, or run away, into some foolish digression. Face this urgency as soon as you notice it and what was an enemy turns into some sensible operation in yourself, of thought or of feeling, for example. As soon as it has turned into such an operation we understand that nothing but our self was the weight, and our self was the enemy. The fool blames, but he is his own enemy. He accuses, but in fact he always accuses himself, without knowing. Or he talks a blue streak and everyone else wishes he would catch himself on and either shut up or talk sense.

This is what it amounts to – we should either shut up or talk sense. Sense is so crucial. Foolishness everywhere abounds. A man of sense stands out like a bulwark, and when he speaks, he does so upon reflection. He is not afraid to stand alone. The pressure that isolates is valuable to him, so he thrives in isolation. Continually and repeatedly he examines himself, inwardly and outwardly, because he is on the look-out for raw-materials.

69

He has joined these others because he wants to help do something and he wants to help get things done that need to be done. There are so many angles to every question. We all arrive at some identified problem from our own unique point of vantage, and this is as it should be. It is a great wonder that there can ever be genuine agreement, on any topic. The agreement is another word for community. It wants to occur to us, this agreement, but it stands to reason that first we have to be changed; we have to undergo change and we have to grow. We are human beings, and problems stimulate our growth. The solutions to those problems, once they occur to us, are signs and warrants that we have in fact changed to the better and grown. Between the problem and the solution lies our advancement. Solutions may be simple or tricky, but they must amount to a transformation of ourselves in unison with the problem. Unless we take the problem on board and thoroughly countenance it as a problem, instead of looking for some shortcut, we cannot have the real benefit of that genuine growth stimulus.

The pressure is physical, the urge is psychic, the problem is mental. All three can be patiently identified in their own original sphere before they become complicated, aggravating, destructive.

The growth stimulus is always there, available in some shape or other. The complication, the aggravation and the destruction, these we cause ourselves. An annoying problem is a mental growth stimulus which we ourselves have complicated. A depression is a physical growth stimulus to which we have not risen. An anxiety is a psychic growth stimulus for which we should have been ready but we were not. We are here to do some work, not to react – to one another or to the fears that leap up in us suddenly and unavoidably. We are here to make sense. This we achieve by identifying continually and repeatedly in fullest possible awareness the problems, urges and pressures that are vouchsafed us, not so that we complain about them but so that we may grow, in community too.

The collective will is not the communal voice. He who would speak with the communal voice must get the collective will under. In himself, nowhere else, can he get it under, this dragon, this mischief, this foolishness.

Who speaks with the communal voice? The one who has managed at any given time to get the collective will under and he does not abuse his readiness of speech but waits for the communal voice to make itself heard.

Another element has been added. The communal voice is ready articulate. You know that you speak while you speak. You see clearly and at the same time you are aware of yourself. There is no agony of expression, but either speech or silence.

We seem to have so much to say, suddenly, when we finally get our say, because the others have stopped and the finger points to us. Whence this rush of words? Why this need for ultimate confession? Every second word says: I am afraid, I am afraid. There is neither time nor room for confession when the time has come to get things done. Many others are waiting for these things to be accomplished and here we sit, trying to explain why we are afraid, justifying ourselves. That is our underlying agenda. On the surface we may be touching on various topics, but in reality we are caught up in our individual psychic complexities. We say nothing clearly. Usually some sort of a complaint shines through. Or a pretentiousness. What is it we do when we 'hold forth'? These are all nervous discharges. We do not want to make sense but to ease our burden, and we try to ease it by unloading it onto those around us who are, as it were, a captive audience. We are going to 'say our piece' because 'we have a right to'. None of this is productive. Constraint comes into the meeting. Many feel tempted to judge and condemn us, which is not good either.

In the absence of pressure, of urgency, of problems, silence is usually of the essence. It might be well to stress one again the virtue of remaining silent. Silence is not an absence of something, but a presence of something. Silence is the presence of actual being, or the actual presence of being. Silence is the womb of the communal voice. Be silent, be still, and know that, in a gathering of several, you make all the while a worthwhile contribution. Be aware of this, otherwise you are only being quiet, which is not the same as being silent. The active contribution of silence is a preparation for the event of the communal voice. 'There was a hush, and then he spoke.'

The collective will is suppressed. There is neither pressure nor an urgency and there are no problems. But you have nothing to say. Should you not have plenty to say now? No, now is the time to be silent, and to keep silent. A problem may present itself yet, or a pressure, before you speak with the communal voice in articulation. You continue to watch for this while you keep silent. But you know all the time that your silence is, in itself, not articulate but in abeyance – and all the while effective. Keep this in mind and remind yourself repeatedly: all the while effective! We can do nothing useful unless we know all the while that it works, even though we may not have any sensible evidence that it does work. There is never any sensible evidence that silence works while it does. So we have to know this from having learned it immediately, or directly, not through our sense but in trust, by trusting.

Silence makes no sense, but it makes many an allowance for sense, and this has to be memorized. Silence is effective communication in that sense. It bridges the intervals between persons. The collective will does exactly the opposite. It divorces person from person. It is always at first an accident and a trap. Then we struggle in that trap, hoping to escape from it by speaking more and more volubly about freedom. But in order to gain freedom we would have to be quiet, then identify the pressure, the urgency, the problem; then deal with these patiently until they were all, so to speak, 'used up', and all this we would accomplish in perfect peace and quiet. Then we might experience the advent of silence, which is like the sunrise after a long night. In peace and quiet we dealt with our problems so that they no longer agitated or appalled us, with our feelings of depression and oppression, so that we no longer fought against them or collapsed under them; with our urgencies, so that they no longer propelled us into precipitate activity or left us in a state of panic. Perhaps we had quite a time with that collective will before it left us room for peace and quiet. It may help to say to it: "Leave me in peace now, I want no more of your self-importance, of your self-pity, of your string of complaints. I have had quite enough of you again. You talk so much because you want to drown out the little sense I have left, so that I will make a complete and utter fool of myself. Be done now!" The rest maybe has to be done by a straightforward assertion of our will to silence. Notice I say 'our' will. The collective will can never be ours. We do not possess it. It possesses us. When that accident once again has occurred due to our lack of attentiveness, we are possessed by the collective will, and if someone afterwards played back to us our obsessive ramblings, given we were now somewhat grown, we would be appalled. "Such horrendous nonsense!" we would cry out. "How could I possibly have been so careless? So irresponsible? So hurtful and damaging to those around me?"

Many, many hours of attentiveness, of making sense in peace and quiet before we open our mouth, many hours of practical silence are of the essence before we can speak maturely, with the communal voice, not tempting but supporting, not offloading but bearing, not seducing but liberating – not trapping but freeing.

What a marvellous adventure is speech! A poet says: "We are a language," and so we are, while we put paid to the collec-

73

tive will and invest in our communal voice. What I do for you while you are trapped is worthwhile for me, of course, so I take care not to chide you, but to bear with you while you are under the sway of this mischief-maker. At such times, how valuable for both of us if I keep silent. Perhaps at another time you will do the same for me. Then gradually we will grow in our communality, never judgmentally, never criticizing, but identifying the signals of growth and good change in one another and helping one another gladly to make sense.

_____ (5/1/'96)

12

What Are Ideas

Ideas are formed in our mind and they take on the form of the human mind willingly. An idea is something that has taken on the form of our human mind, but what this something is has never been properly pinpointed, because one has always attempted to look at ideas in general from the point of view of other ideas, and no matter how brilliantly this has been done, the point of vantage was not the right one. It was as if one were hopeful to become acquainted with the essence of the temporal life from the point of view of death, which death can of course only be part and parcel of that same temporal life. No, in order to gain a helpful perspective one would have to make one's inquiry on the basis not of an aspect of the temporary, but of eternal life, and those who have not yet achieved a possession here will always seem to be describing the outside of a prison building from within a locked cell.

Ideas are attracted to our mind due to its readiness for change. When we usually speak of a change of mind we mean a decision or conviction exchanged for another, but this is not intended here when we speak of our mind's readiness for change. Think of your mind as the totality of all your outward

74

perceivable functions. I am aware of your mind when I observe how you move, how the gestures of your face come and go, how the words you speak relate to the entire impression you make on me. Commonly 'the mind' is imagined as somehow invisible inside us, as a secret faculty over which we have more or less control. But truly we have no control over our mind, only over our self or ego, and this is of doubtful benefit, because why should we wish to manipulate the thing we would be better off without?

The mind as inside us and as invisible, when we view it in perspective, turns out to be something like a reflex, or even a cramp of our ego. Really I cannot make very much at all of my own mind because it exists, and comes into existence, precisely for your sake, so that you may come to know me. Once I am truly in the possession of my mind I am offering it to you, as myself become visible. You perceive me in terms and by means of my mind.

We cannot know what ideas truly are until we come into the proper possession of our mind. Until then we are under the influence of ideas and in a sense subservient to them, without being entirely aware of this. In that case the pleasure we associate with the manipulation of ideas and with the sense of power we derive from it is decidedly egocentric. We suppose that we ourselves are in the driver's seat. In fact our ego makes the moves, while using and abusing us to gain its ends and meanwhile rewarding us with little pleasures. No matter how inflated these pleasures become, they are still little, so that this egocentric ideality must take its toll. And it does take its toll, whether we combine it with morality and beliefs or simply with a criminal or foolish self-gratification.

We have to be very careful now when we inquire into what we suppose is the cause of this egocentric ideality. Since we do not initially choose it, we are apt to project benevolent or malevolent forces as causes, and perhaps we turn these into myths and imagine them as personal agents. This is most usual and common. We speak of a climate of ideas, of an ideal cultural context, and the like. But as soon as we approach this question of the cause of ideas responsibly we must admit that ideas simply happen to us, and that we can no more initiate them than we can lift ourselves off the ground by our hair. What does make all the difference in the world however is the time of this happening – or of these accidents.

And here we return to our original view of our human mind as the visible means of ourselves, by which we offer ourselves to one another in the light of day. Now any ideas that happen to us during the course of such communality can in fact be called happy ideas, since they correspond to the happiness of our state of being, attesting to it and reflecting it. While we own our mind and make use of it in accordance with its definition as the means at our disposal for loving communality, ideas come into being in a surprising fashion, and in essence they perfect, as it were from without, our communal humanity. We might care to imagine them as agents of grace. Through them we know that our happiness overflows. We may think them through and feel the consequences of this, which eventually amounts to a habit of perfection and completion – not for me individually by myself in a corner, in private, for the sake of public acclaim, but always and again for us. Real ideas, happy ideas, cannot occur to anyone except under such conditions of mature responsibility, once we have come to realize that we can truly live for one another and not I for myself and you for your self.

A real idea operates like a seal, and as a seal. When I say that we think such ideas through I mean directly, with the power of our spirit, in order to realize them, so that they no longer exist then as ideas. Our openness to such ideas is nothing in addition to our communal behaviour as we exist for one another.

When I say that we feel the consequences of such ideas I mean once again that we feel directly what comes along rather than letting it degenerate as bad feeling, as disappointment, perplexity or heaviness of spirit. These ideas are to become real as ourselves, in terms of our mind <u>and</u> of our body, so the feeling we do is as important as the thinking, and we should never suppose that feeling, emotion and passion contribute less than thought to ourselves as living beings.

In the light of this it would seem that what is generally called an idea is not a true idea at all but something immature or premature. When we do not yet take the responsibility for our mind we are naturally inclined to look only after our own interests, or only after someone else's interest, so that we become selfish or sacrificial, neither of which can lead to a realization of ourselves. The mind we use then is not ours at all and the thinking we do is more like a sifting of opinions. What happens then is that we are motivated in a way that is to bring home to us the fact of our imperfection so that we might seek perfection. Unless we actively seek perfection we are bound to misapprehend what comes our way. The idle or grasping hands of our bare individuality misconceive what the diligent and patient hands of ourselves as persons would correctly identify. Egocentric ideas are therefore formed not by our mind, and they do not show or testify to the shape of our mind but, since we really have no mind of our own, they are more or less products of our immaturity or of our prematurity, presented to us, not so that we should continue to be misinformed, but so that we might recognize our stage and state. What is commonly done with these so-called ideas however is more like self-aggrandizement and world-abuse. As a result the misconception increases. It amounts to something like a misappropriation of funds. We seem to sense that the mind we use is not our own, so we try to make up for it by possessing these unhappy ideas. We call them our own, guard them jealously, take out patents and copyrights and trade on them to put money in our pockets. What we forfeit is mature human being and community.

It must seem nearly impossible for anyone in the bad habit of misconceiving imperfect ideas to understand what is meant here by a true idea. And yet there slumbers in him a desire for perfection and a longing for being complete. If this desire and longing could be awakened, which can only be managed by way of beauty and love, all egocentric ideas would appear repulsive and hateful and a revolution in thinking and feeling would be brought about. The very disagreeableness and unpleasantness of these ideas would then affect us in such a way that we might possibly regret our present mental state and begin to reflect. All depends now on how successful we are in liberating ourselves from the influence of all these egocentric ideas. The most effective method is repentance, but an egocentric idea of repentance is usually all that is available. Certainly we cannot use any of these ideas in order to rid ourselves of them. And the logic of perfection is beyond us. It would seem that wherever we turn we are trapped by our own mental products. Meditation and contemplation might help us, depending again, however, on how we go about it.

It cannot be our own mind until we are rid of all egocentric ideas. It is not a case of our mind being a container in which one content is to be replaced by another. All there is of a mind in us is in fact these egocentric ideas, so getting rid of these means getting rid of what we mean by our mind.

We might try concentrating on our body and leaving all mental activity aside. Vision, in other words feeling, emotion and passion, shall involve us entirely. 'Cleanse your eye and your body is full of light.' Take an interest in the appearance of the world around you, the world in all its variety and manifold beauty. Gaze at all things natural in the knowledge that this will transfer their essence to you. The essence of being is humanity. Do not gaze dumbly, like a fool, but in the knowledge of what goes on while you gaze. Behold the cloudy sky, the material earth, the starry universe. As you do this, and after some time of it, you gradually become aware of who you are, and of the fact that you are someone. Now all these things will speak to you with a voice that at once will be your voice and you will recognize how all that lives is linked in a chain of magnificent being. You will sense the proximity of your creator as often as you choose and as intimately as you care. Ideas are so far from your mind that you have no mind worth mentioning. Your body is your medium. You are acquiring a body of knowledge. Be careful not to insult with your intellect what you see and hear. Keep your intellect entirely subservient to the faculty of vision, namely to feeling, emotion and passion. But you will get swamped by sensation and overwhelmed by feeling if you do not continually and repeatedly acknowledge that what goes on while you gaze and behold is a transfer of humanity from created reality to you in person. Attest to this eventually by giving of your life to others. Do not be afraid if you feel depleted. This is a sign that you are being filled.

So we may come to life not by way of our mind but of our body, and if all our mental activity has in the past been idealized we may let go of it entirely and use our bodily functions instead, such as seeing, hearing, feeling, being glad and passionate.

After a time we will have our own body, which means that we may see or not see, feel or not feel, as we choose, and our body will have become productive. We will be able to appeal to the feeling, emotion and passion of others, especially of those who are beset by premature and immature ideas, to the detriment of their human being.

Due to our communal activity, once we have become sufficiently secure in it, we become accessible then to true ideas, which will not remind us at all of the idealized mentality we have left behind. These true ideas become the building of our mind. They add up, link up, relate and associate, in such a fashion that our mind is the counterpart of our body and totally in step with it. We are then not any more capable of untrue ideas and this is a tremendous relief to us. Our new mind – this is what we may call it. It is capable of all those functions and of only those functions which at one time seemed unattainable to us except perhaps in something we called, in our false resignation, the afterlife. But if that idealized mentality was life, then this now is indeed the afterlife, though in fact it is life, while then we knew only self-indulgence and strife.

True ideas make up what we mean by our mind. What we have patiently suffered, seen through and thought through, is perfected by more and more ideas which come into being as soon as we are ready for them and prior to that they do not exist. As soon as they exist they are my or your individuality, part of it and the whole of it. We have access to them then in a variety of ways, but chiefly they show what we are so far.

_____   (18/9/'96)

13

Our New Mind

Our new mind, corresponding to our new body, is the sum-total of all of our true ideas, and at the same time each of these ideas is our entire mind. How can this be explained? The difficulty arises only if we picture these ideas, as somehow separate from a human being. But of course they do not exist except as the mind of a human being. So we really have to ask: What is our mind? Or: How are we different when we have a mind of our own?

I am not going to discuss 'the' mind here, or anything mental or ideal at all except insofar as it belongs to someone, is owned or possessed by someone. As people we are actually possessed by a mind and find ourselves at the mercy of ideas which are not true. None of this will concern us here. Only true ideas interest us, and our new mind.

If we have a mind it must be visible to all and sundry. But then it is not our mind which is visible but we ourselves as human beings. A human being is visible because of his mind. We watch how he behaves, we listen to him speak. A human being is always someone in action. Even if he sleeps, then that is what he does. A mind is at work. And yet it is the human being himself. How can we explain that?

The difficulty arises if we try to picture a being with a mind as compared to a being without a mind. There is no such thing as a human being without a mind. Let us put it this way: By way of his mind a human being extends into the light of day. We cannot say that he is his mind, this would be incorrect. Which brings home to us forcibly that every human being exists in community. Community is the necessary context of all human beings; they never exist in isolation. What we picture is necessarily always out of any context and in isolation. So we cannot picture human beings in any case, only people. If we can picture something, it is not a human being.

A human being by definition stands in community with other human beings and it is this communal aspect which we mean by his mind. I perceive you as a human being because of your mind and ... because you exist communally, by the necessity that makes out your freedom. I can see you, not your flesh, and I can hear you, not your voice, because of your mind. You, not our torso, arms, legs and head only, are visible to me because of your mind.

We come face to face here with the great mystery that is every human being. We make no bones about it, human beings are difficult to grasp as entities in themselves, and this is so because we cannot perceive them except in relation to ourselves. Thankfully this is so. Accustomed as we perhaps are to popular wisdom, this may strike us as a hindrance or as due to a shortcoming in ourselves, but when we look at the 'humanities', as they are called, and at the study of 'man', we find here precisely the isolation at work that pertains to people, who escape from freedom, and not to human beings, who are bound to be free. They are bound by their communality to be free. They have found their way back to one another and they forge as many links as possible to chain themselves to one another.

Ideas are rewards. We behave virtuously, manfully, for example, so that we may have more mentality, among other things. If I find myself hating you and then love you instead, intentionally, this is bound to result in ideas, in something else which is life that is added on to us. More life is what we want. More ideas, a greater mind, means more life. The greater our mind the more powerfully we live.

When human beings think, they do something for one another. I am thinking at the moment, and if you were here beside me you would see me writing my thought down. The thinking does not go on inside my head, like an alchemical reaction, but it goes on as my writing. I think of nothing separate from or in addition to my writing. I may momentarily stare into space, or scratch my head, or squeeze my eyes shut because it is late and they hurt, but then this too is my mind – unless of course I do it absent-mindedly. If I do, I have something to catch up, which will once again by my mind at work, or me at work in terms of, or by way of, my mind.

Another way of looking at it reveals to me my own mind as what I wish to reveal of myself to you. I want to show you what I mean, and this is my way of revealing to you not something from me but me myself. Communication takes place because each one of us wants to show something of himself to the other. Your laughter communicates your joy, your tears your sorrow. You extend your right hand towards me as we meet. Your face is beaming with the pleasure of recognition – or closed off on account of an apprehension.

The question arises as to why we should bother speaking of a mind at all, once we are rid of that ego-equipment by which we were wont to steer our course from shoal to reef and back again. Certainly something has changed since then. Once we were busy in our heads, to the detriment of our hearts, or vice versa.

We could never quite get the two together. Are we afraid of sliding back into that unenviable state of affairs? Is our talk of a new mind now an insurance to keep us on the straight and narrow?

But we have come through the strait and narrow. It seems we can relax now and exercise our new mind, as in a new heaven, just as we can behave with our bodies, as on a new earth. What, if anything, are we worried about?

It has to do with communication. I want to let you know what I mean so that you too may choose human being with all your heart and soul and strength. It concerns me that you are not fully in the possession of your mind. So naturally I have to describe myself in terms at least partially familiar to you. For that reason and for no other, I speak of my mind. It would suit me simply to be who I am, but then I do work. I come out of myself, I extend myself towards you. I give you the benefit of some of my ideas, and this is of equal benefit to me, because my mind quite naturally goes out towards you.

When I use my mind, when I think, I bring to awareness, both of myself and others, certain connections, contacts and associations, by which I, as a human being, am related to other beings. These relations are worth bringing out into the open, where other human beings can then enjoy the reality of them. I am thinking right now. If you observe carefully what goes on here you will know what I mean by my mind. The old thinking went on 'in my head', whatever that means. There was, in any case, no outward evidence of it. "Think before you speak!" we are told. That is the old thinking. The new thinking is: "Speak when you think." The new thought is always right away acted out. When you observe how a human being behaves – which is bound to be a loving observation, by the way, not clinical or critical – you have to give a name, or rather you might like to give a name, to the one thing that goes into all this behaviour and embraces it. That is thought. And the thought is the human being inasmuch as there is this demonstration of himself, this visible example of singular and specific humanity. You can say: "He does this and behaves like that," but that will be more like you impartially looking at him, not engaging, communicating with him. "He is speaking in short sentences," you say. "He walks with a secure step. When he turns his head he seems a little stiff in the neck. Now he smiles and helps a child into a seat." But go a bit further now. Take another step towards him. Become aware of the bond of humanity between you, of the relation called human being, and now two things happen – you look for a name for all that visible wealth of life, and you notice how that person becomes identifiable 'in the round', as a whole being, not just as someone who shows you a single aspect of himself and all you can know is that aspect. It is true that he does show you an aspect of himself, but if you know the thought you have the benefit of the whole being

People are not to be perceived this way. But imagine the disappointment if a human being came along and you lacked the equipment for the perception! Would you ever forgive yourself? The experience would leave you feeling hollow in the stomach and heavy on the brain. So take no risks. Practice thoughtful seeing now. Study this notion of a person's mind as thought in action demonstrating and illustrating that human being for you in a way that gives you that whole person, which really is marvellous.

Do not be afraid of losing track of old and familiar characteristics. That dear face you know so well – it will return, but much fleshed out by spirit, and you yourself will have much more of that hindrance removed in you that judges by appearances. While we focus on appearances we never get to know more than details for a while. Look for the thought, for the mind, and sure enough you have to let go of those familiar details if they have not yet gone mouldy, but keep in mind they return transformed and eternal in a setting of thought. Humanity is the essence of being. Whatever is, is human. There are beings we call human beings, which sounds superficially repetitive; in fact what we have here is beings who are aware of themselves, and therefore in a unique way of one another. One such way we describe when we speak of our mind, of our new mind, and of the thought that means it.

Can I not get to know you directly? Do I need to focus on your mind in order to see you? Why can I not see you immediately?

So much confusion is evident in those questions, and above all once again this is due to the bad habit of picturing what cannot be pictured, of using that old mind, with is customary 'inside-the-head' activities. Come out of your head and think in the light of day. Let the light of day into your head. As soon as you argue or enquire according to some picture you are on the wrong track, on the track of infidelity. When pictures occur to us, let's not get entangled in them with our old mind but let us simply let them be while we think outside our heads instead. Clear your eye of all pictures, on the other hand, by wishing to do so, for the perfectly good reason of your entire body full of light.

Our new mind is visible for all who have eyes to see and ears to hear, in other words, of all who have a new body. We cannot lastingly appreciate appearance in detail while we concentrate on one at a time and ignore that which reveals itself to us by way of these details; that which is entailed by these details.

And we do well to begin with human beings, because there our perception is most successfully rewarded. There we have to do with actual thought and with an imperative mind. Then we may proceed to other beings, to animals, plants and minerals, and finally even to elements. What interests us always and everywhere is our true relation to all that is. There is endless joy in an endless task and many may benefit from our labours.

Why would we not be as diligent as possible in exploring the world with our new mind? Would we rather remain each one in his own dark corner, fighting to establish a relation that has long ago been established and insisting on individual tendencies at the expense of personhood? We cannot derive the reality of our surroundings from our own delusions. No matter how vibrant, picturesque and dear to us these delusions have become, as we cosset and pamper them with centre-stage attention, still the communal element is lacking, and without it, whether by private means or to public ends, we can never be whole, for our vision is not whole, and for what is whole we lack the perception.

——————— (20/1/'96)

14

The Communal Element

It might be possible to establish something like a doctrine of the elements. What are they, these elements, in any case? Can two or three of us mean the same thing when we use that word? Through the ages one or two interpretations have found traditional favour.

The smallest possible constituent of reality – this would be a new way of looking at it – depending on what we mean by reality. The downward spiral from human beings through animals, plants and minerals, might be seen to end in – not 'the' elements, which feels more like a mythic than a scientific entity, but in elements. If we say 'the elements' we have a finite sum of them in mind, but imagined, and there we have often in our writings spoken of the five elements: earth, air, fire, water and sun. Another way of looking at it is not through the imagination but purely for the sake of our understanding, and there we will try to make some new sense now of what we mean by elements. We choose not to use a dictionary or an encyclopaedia to help us out, because we want to arrive at an entirely new performance of this word. Meanwhile it may be necessary to glance at what we will call – for the moment only perhaps but maybe for all time – the spiral of creation. Let's see what happens. Ideas will assist us when the time for them is ripe.

A scientific definition of a spiral is a point that moves through concentric circles along a path. The notion of forward motion is combined with the idea of circular constraint. That the one is a notion and the other an idea is of interest, because the notion involves our body while the idea implies our individuality. nothing less than the union and consummation of our body and our mind comes into play here.

We come up with a notion of something due to our capacity for sense and feeling, so a notion is an element of our body, namely of our body of knowledge. An idea occurs to us, as an element of our thinking mind, as soon as the conditions for it exist.

Now all created beings have this in common, that they have been created and that they participate in creation. The fact that they have been created lends them a historic dimension, and this we are glad to take into account when we contemplate these beings so as to become aware of our relationship. We have come into being, at one time, and so have they. A horse, a dandelion, a quartz crystal – an element: they have all begun, and so have we. But the fact that, like ourselves, they participate in creation, makes them co-owners, with us, of mutual experience. We experience them and they, in their own way, experience us, and this experience is something that conditions and – cushions. Those who lack this experience are not at home on the earth. Those who have a little of it usually go out of their way to look for more. They have discovered that they belong on the earth, and that all these other beings belong on the earth, and ... that there is a communal element.

This communal element is always the first one among elements to be discovered. It represents the quintessential nature of belonging. We have to have looked at a few things with an eye to their innermost being before we can even begin to wonder, to question: Is there not something that allows all these beings somehow to fit? A thing is not known to us until we discover that it is. Then its being, or even the fact that it is, interests us or causes us a measure of disquiet, so consequently we say: 'Let there be a meeting and a greeting!'. Then there is a moment of recognition. We have known each other all along, without realizing it. The process of realization has started. Another relationship is coming to our awareness and we encourage that as best we can. We fit, both one another and into a common context. The communal element is being brought to our attention. Once it has come to our attention a few times we may have to go through a period of desertion and homelessness before we begin properly to appreciate this communal element, so that we will not wait for it any more to come to us, but, like mature human beings, we take steps to come to it. This is a joyful turn off affairs indeed.

But what are we saying here: the communal element? What is it? Is it some sort of an experience? Can we build on it? Can we isolate it, objectify it, give it some other name? Where and how does it exist? Does it exist at all?

There is more to human beings than meets the eye, that much is clear. Animals are fairly obvious. Plants, in turn dip down into the dream world in a strange way. Minerals are difficult. We need to be happy with the surface of them, because that is all there is, just surface. But elements are nameless. They make up the root, the source, the origin of things, and while we cannot imagine them away, we sense that if they were not, nothing would be. Among all the created beings, these are the ones that are only perceived, not perceived here or there, now and then. They are moments of perception.

For example, when I perceive the element of communality, or the communal element, I have, as it were, a key in my hand that allows me to unlock the doors between beings. I do perceive this element, but because it is a moment of perception, I right away also have something in my hand, something I can work with, apply, draw on.

But I will have to get away from mistaking this element for anything other than a token of perception, for that is what it remains to me, though it points to the communal connection of all beings in reality. It is my earnest of that connection, and my hold on that relationship. On one hand I have to guard against the materialistic notion that it binds beings together, as though it constituted some kind of cosmic cement, while on the other hand I do well to steer clear of the idealism of seeing in it a sort of magic wand in my hand, with which I can cause beings to reveal to me their heart of hearts. The way we all fit in one context of being, this is the truth of the matter that has us intrigued and keeps our hand on the tiller of live knowledge, and as soon as we have this element of communality in our perceptive possession, we need no longer wonder: "Do all beings fit into our human scale of perception or is an essential link still missing which we cannot supply?" and we no longer suspect that: "This truth I perceive may perhaps be only subjective; or exclusively objective, so that although it exists, what good is that to me?" No, I know that the subject in this case, with a little bit of urging, reveals to me the object, and that the object, with a modicum of study, reveals itself gladly as subject.

So what we are getting at here is a way of experiencing reality through created beings, and a key being we have identified is the communal element. It sounds odd, of course, to call an element a being, because we think of beings as entire each onto itself while elements are usually imagined as inert building blocks. However the imagined elements are not what we want here. We are speaking of something that can be perceived. We literally mean experience as perception. And the hallmark of perception is that we begin with an understanding of our union with what we perceive. So perception is neither objective nor subjective. It is, after all, knowledge of beings by human beings. We, who are beings, are getting to know other beings. Naturally you would expect that we do not treat these beings as things, as objects of curiosity, distancing ourselves from them inwardly, or as subjects, lording it over them. The onus is on ourselves then to learn proper perception.

An element, such as this cumulative element, is not a thing, not something we can do justice to by treating it as though it were a thing. We may take it for granted that since it is, it has something to tell us, to relate to us. Animals, plants and minerals have something to relate to us, if only we have the ears to perceive. The relation is different with each, but also in an essential way the same with all, including human beings.

Our relation to the communal element is easy. Here we have something that is real though it does not appear. While we try to come to terms with some appearance of it we fail. However, whatever other being we intend to perceive, we will not succeed here either unless we take this communal element into account. When we view the ascending spiral of creation, all lower ranks are contained in every higher one. And in human beings we find all other beings, including this communal element, presented, in a way that has not yet been discussed. And in a human being reality fully and completely appears. So we may ask: How can we, in whom reality fully appears, contain an aspect of reality that does not appear? This communal element is after all present in us after a fashion. Should we speak of elemental reality? Of vegetal and animal reality? How can we come to terms with this knowledge of our all-inclusive human being, with this singular experience of recognition when we view animals, plants, minerals and elements? Evidently these other creatures afford us opportunities of learning about ourselves, by drawing us out of ourselves and helping us to know ourselves in the light of day.

This business of coming out into the light of day is of crucial importance for all human beings, because here finally they may become fully aware of their stature and station and rank. In the light of day all relationships work. We are after all related to all other beings not so that we may explain ourselves or our environment, but so that we may have an abundance of life. So when we say that all relationships work in the light of day, this in itself is sufficient reason for coming into the light of day. A working relationship implies a replenishing and a profusion of life.

Our working relationship in the light of day with the communal element ensures us a degree of communality in awareness with all beings, including human beings. Perceive this element more diligently and strengthen the relationship.

All elements have been created and participate in creation, but in their case these two aspects, or sides, cannot be told apart. We may assume them. Cosmically they have been created and universally they participate in creation. We are fortunate to be able to perceive them from both sides, though due to their nature, due to the way they come into being, we have no way of appreciating both facets simultaneously, as we have with all other beings, and as we are required to do if we are to appreciate the true nature of human beings.

As soon as we speak of the nature, rather than of the reality of beings, we choose, as it were, a double stance vis-à-vis their being, and, mindful of their reality, we must consider their nature as twofold. The choice to consider the nature, rather than right away the reality of every being, has to do again, as we mentioned at the beginning, with our willingness to assist one another towards perfection and wholeness. The step from nature to reality is fraught with pitfalls. The most dangerous of these is the tacit assumption that there is no such thing as the reality that embraces all things natural, so that the mere appearance of the world is mistaken for reality and therefore either demonized or rejected.

Therefore we do well to assist one another through this critical passage from nature to reality, from individuality to personality. Only those who know reality, having experienced it, can

91

help those who are still largely enthralled by their twofold nature and who are therefore in need, often in dire need, of being rescued. A relationship with someone who is really intact is of the essence for them.

The perception of reality through created beings allows us to number among those beings elements, such as the communal element, and to step into relation with them. We can, however, only do this for one another. On behalf of one another we can step into an elementally real relationship, especially by perceiving this communal element. I cannot do it on my own. On behalf of you I may bring this element to my awareness and make the relationship work for both of us. Again we can see how this can be called the key element. We ourselves can have the benefit of it only while we use it to unlock doors to reality for others.

And the implications for our faculty of perception in general would seem obvious. Unless we love we have no part of reality, neither in mind nor in body. That true perception must be a loving activity goes without saying. Our perception of elements, especially of this communal element, is fundamental to our perception of reality through all other created beings, and we cannot be at home on the earth except in creative working relationships with other created beings, especially human beings.

(22/1/'96)

15

The Spiral of Creation

All created beings stand in relation to one another. Since all beings are created, it suffices that we speak of beings, since their creation is implied.

The classification of beings embraces only minerals, plants and animals, not elements and human beings. All five cannot be grouped under one concept; in other words, they are not all classes, or species.

We call it the 'spiral' of creation because this helps us to think through how elements undergo a metamorphosis during relationship; how minerals undergo a transformation and plants a transubstantiation during relationship; how animals undergo a transmutation and human beings undergo change during relationship. All of these relationships imply a change but in the case of human beings this change cannot be specified in an way.

Now we need to be aware of what is meant by change in all these cases, and how relationship entails it. Models will help us understand. An element in relationship with another element changes in such a way that it can be perceived more clearly by us on account of its characteristics to which we may subscribe. The metamorphosis has nothing to do with appearances, since elements do not appear, but it refers to a change in the way we are bound to approach it. Remember that all beings exist in relation, and that we may bring this more or less to our awareness, perceptively. We do not do something so as to enter into this relation; what we do, as perception, lets us know what is going on and where we stand in any case, and this is our aim: to be much more aware of our fortunate position as human beings, and of our responsibility, if not obligation, to all other beings. For the way we relate to another being, once we have become somewhat aware of our relationship with it, is quite different to the way we co-exist with it indifferently and in ignorance due to a lack of such perceptive awareness.

Specific about metamorphosis is that characteristics are removed and renewed. Consider for example the communal element. Its characteristics at a given moment may include intelligent wisdom and compassionate care. During our awareness in relationship we know this – and then we have known it, so that it has become a part of our body of knowledge and is no longer accessible to our thought. As soon as we reapply ourselves however, we may discover the next set of characteristics, such as unfailing courage and tactful propriety. During the working relationship the first two have become – have changed into – the next two. Or consider the <u>cumulative element</u>. At a given moment of perception the overriding characteristic by which we know this element and relate to it may be successful progress. This suits us fine while it lasts, but then it is no longer available to us. If we have some insight into element-metamorphosis we are not dismayed by this but instead we get ready for the new characteristic, which in this case is steady increase. We cannot predict the next characteristic, only that there will be one. All change, in that general sense, is predictable.

When we speak of the metamorphosis of elements in relationship, we certainly have no notion, or desire to know, of anything that goes on independently from us as perceptive beings. Therefore it remains all the same whether we mean the relationship of one element with another or of an element with an animal or with ourselves as aware human beings. Working relationships are drawn to our attention and become the aim of our compassionate curiosity.

None of these working relationships can be perceived in our minds but always in the light of day. We perceive in the light of day and it makes out the sum-total of our awareness. Remember that daylight exists outside of us, but we exist in the light of day, so take care not to confuse the two.

The transformation of minerals, now, is nothing to do with characteristics but with shape. This demonstrates for us how elements participate in minerals. A change of shape is gradual, not abrupt. Also a tangible by-product accompanies every such change. Elements do not appear, but minerals appear to be. We think of them as anchored in appearance. Coal and petroleum are minerals, for example, and they exist in transformation in the sense that we can never perceive them in a state. Of course we tend to view them statically but we do well to overcome this tendency, just as we do well to overcome our tendency to view elements as sporadic and arbitrary. The process of renewal during metamorphosis must be recognized and acknowledged by us, therefore, and in the case of transformation we must take account of the fact that the tangible by-product is not the mineral itself.

The tangible by-product is the type of mineral we find. There are many types of coal, or of stone. What counts is not that we differentiate these types precisely, but that we keep in mind what it is we have found, namely a type of mineral, not the mineral itself, which exists in constant gradual transformation.

Minerals, then, are natural by-products of transformation. We cannot call them actual products, because that would imply that a transformation process ends in a mineral, which is decidedly not the case. A mineral is known to us in a twofold way, as transformation and as a given by-product. We cannot know the by-product until we identify in ourselves that aspect of change which in the case of minerals is transformation. Human beings have the unique capacity to transcend. All being, all that is, is human, but not all beings are human. Think what this means. We have what it takes to know all other beings due to this transcendability, due to this fact, first of all, that our own changing is greater than the changing of all other beings, so that we can readily recognize, metamorphosis, transformation, transubstantiation and transmutation. Not only can we recognize but we can empathize. In ourselves we suffer creation itself, hence we are able to suffer all creations. All that matters is that we come down from our various levels of abstraction and entrust ourselves perceptively to the realm of creations. The abstraction removed us from mere things, and this has been crucial. But the purpose of this abstraction – since abstraction is nothing in itself but a means to an end – has always been not the fabrication of novelties but our re-entry into the realm of creation, where we may be at home on earth.

Moving on to the transubstantiation of plants now we come to the conclusion here that plant life is in fact substantial, but only to the extent that we can detect an underlying movement of parts. We are familiar with the various parts of plants and with the way in which each is contained in the previous. We are able to follow what can be described as a transformation of parts, but at the same time we know of a metamorphosis of the whole. So we recognize in plants also that which gives rise to minerals and that which characterizes elements.

But the transubstantial essence of plants leaves us in no doubt as to the use we can make of plants, and of 'plant-life', for the purpose of furthering our insight into our psychic make-up. A working relationship with plants encourages us first of all to identify within ourselves our tendencies and inclinations. We find ourselves obliged to come up with something fundamental in ourselves if we are not to be overwhelmed psychically by the substance that 'flows' periodically from plants. We experience plants in this way , and even as one plant, one variety or species varies from another, so does this substance again vary, more or less, and each time we experience a more or less different effect on our physical system that urges us to make a sound response, not according to concepts but immediately from our nerves.

Here we see illustrated the <u>transcendence</u> inherent in every working relationship between beings. A spark leaps across the individual divide. The relation of beings transcends their individuality, so that they may come out of themselves into the light of day.

In plants this transcendence may be observed as one stage of plant growth succeeds another and as we ourselves leave ourselves open to the influence of stimuli from there. A transubstantial change occurs in our psychic make-up, as a consequence of which we become more aware of our psyche, which is always useful, since then we are empowered to do work, even in terms of our soul.

The problem with plants is always that we suppose ourselves ill used if we cannot right away make external observations. But the emphasis in this relation is always in the realm of he psychic, where we struggle in our individuality and with our individuality, supposedly on account of, and in terms of, a transfer of substance, but really because nothing has been done by us yet to usher into our system a perfectly natural stimulus that will do us good. External observation gets in the way of this, so that the substantial stimuli accumulate, or pile up. We are consequently under pressure. Relief comes as soon as we perform the necessary act of acceptance. The individual creature then stands on an equal footing with us and the relation works.

Animals undergo a transmutation in relation. Remember, we do not bring about the relation but we can become aware of it, and then it not only works, but it works for us. Animals are related to us not so much in the realm of the psyche but within the context of our existence, our being around, being here or there. Note, once again, that we do not speak of 'the animal', any more than we spoke of 'the plant' above. Animals exist for us in the sense that a non-essential existence is demonstrated and in that existence as such is emphasized for us. Again we can see how this serves to draw us out of our individual self. The possibility and practicality of our own human existence is pointed out to us due to this relation. We become aware here how all other beings are related to us in such a way that we are, so to speak, reminded by them of our inborn freedom, and so that we learn to live freely and then let all those other beings have the advantage of that. So creatures and beings are around us not only so that we will have the benefit of them, but also so that they can then take advantage of what we with their help achieve, on the basis of human freedom. Technically we should view all created beings in such a way that we learn to distinguish between them as they are when we neglect their relation to us and as they are when we shower them with our human freedom. People see in creatures only entities to exploit. But people are out for survival, not life. They know nothing of life. In order that they themselves should survive, everything around them must be reduced to those same rigours and routines of survival, so in consequence nothing can live and has only the choice to die more or less painfully or to attain for a time to the perverse pleasures of mere survival. So we cannot learn anything from the popular point of view. If that view has been foisted on us and then we discover our humanity, we may have, for a while, a hard time of it as we learn the ins and outs of human change and as we become increasingly aware of our creative relationship with all beings. The fact that 'a gulf has been fixed' between us and people strikes us at first with dismay and we may attempt, in our dismay, to make humanistic accommodations because it seems to us that the truth is too hard. Humanism traditionally is invented by us as a consolation over the uncountenanced difference between the quick and the dead. But closing our eyes will not help.

Not that people are entirely defined by the fact that they lack life. The essence of popularity lies elsewhere. As we move along what we have called the spiral of creation, away from animals now and into the fellowship of human beings, we discover that people have in fact opted out of that spiral of creation. They have stepped out of all and any relation with beings and have decided on a substitute, on a replacement, set up in opposition to human creativity and to creative being. We touch here on a matter not merely of neglect and avoidance but of rebellion and usurpation.

Our relationship with other human beings, now, is such that we undergo change, and this constant change is our immunity vis-à-vis people. They are with us only until all these things have come true. Perhaps we should think of them as counter-productive of human change. Of the essence meanwhile of course is our concentration on actual human fellowship, so that we are not deceived into a sidetrack by various modern or even post-modern attempts at a humanistic fudging of the issues. Our business is to love one another, especially when we dislike or even hate one another, and to take great care when people like us and make much of us.

This change we undergo is our happiness, and from the point of view of such constant change we may readily perceive what all other beings undergo, in a sense on behalf of us, but then equally of course for the sake of what can only accrue to them from free and perceptive human beings.

_____   (24/1/'96)

16

The Element of Accumulation

All too often we do the right thing but we have not in mind what we gain by doing it. We gain it alright then, but not for use, only in our sleep as it were, and then we are forced to give it up. For example, we may set out to explore some aspect of reality so as to gain knowledge. If this knowledge merely excites us, how can we later make use of it? It has not become part of us. While we accumulate knowledge, it must be part of our knowledge and an aspect of our knowing, that we do accumulate it. Otherwise we only rid ourselves of riches.

'What we know in our heart,' this refers to the element of accumulation. Here we understand something that can only be understood, it cannot be known. 'What we know in our heart' is what we perceive or understand of our being.

Elements cannot be sensed, or known, only perceived, or understood. Instead of sensation there is belief. Instead of knowledge there is faith. What counts here for our purpose is that no body is required, so that even if our body should be dead, we may still have the benefit of these elements, such as the communal element, of which we have written, and now the cumulative element. These elements are entities of faith, and even as faith (not _a_ faith) is fundamental to knowledge, so are these elements, (not _the_ elements) basic to all being.

This element of accumulation now plays into our recognition of the fact that while we do we gain. Leave to one side for the moment what it is we gain and only consider that something accumulates for us while we are active. As soon as you accept this, but not before, you have the right to ask: "Where do I gain it, and how can I make use of it afterwards?" as soon as you accept that you gain something while you do something, you are on course for in fact gaining it in what we shall for the moment call the realm of conscious reality. In fact you would be smarter to say that you gain in fact such a realm of conscious reality. It comes into being for you and grows. It widens and deepens.

Now this realm of conscious reality is what you might call the optimum condition for life. We cannot do better than that if we want life, and if we want an abundance of it. We know fine well that we cannot create life, or cause it, or bring it about. Life comes to us to the extent that the condition for its arrival is right, and it remains with us on condition that we exist in a certain way.

We cannot imagine elements. It would be silly to try to do so. No bodily characteristics adhere to them. But our faithful perception of them reveals them to us as beings in their own right, which are therefore able to do us more good than we know. If this sounds fanciful, consider how we ourselves, as human beings, stand immersed in cosmic reality that is naturally limitless. Our perception of ourselves as human beings necessitates even from the outset the imposition of a limit. As reality comes into being for us, more and more do such limits and their definitions become crucial for us. What we do, in this way of limiting and defining, makes it possible for reality to achieve its aim with us. We desire, in our deepest nature, to be influenced by this reality. Our definition of an element, now, such as the cumulative element, allows for such an influence. We create the condition for it, so that it may happen.

More specifically now, this cumulative element comes particularly into being in response to our perception of our human being as favoured and at a distinct advantage. We may say that it comes into being <u>for us</u> as soon as we realize that in comparison to all other beings, we human beings are select and choice, and endowed with a special nature. And we may keep this in mind. We may behave in such a way that all other beings in our vicinity, human or otherwise, are sensibly persuaded of our exceptional rank.

This exceptional rank brings with it exceptional risk. If we do not live up to what it means to be a human being, we sink lower than any other being and become, so to speak, unbeings, or things. Now we can imagine ourselves forever involved in a struggle between rank and risk, between what we <u>must</u> achieve and what <u>might</u> happen to us if we do not. But this human approach is modern and needs to be revised. At the centre of this modern approach to life an attitude of 'no pain, no gain' sums up a great deal of what is best but can never be good. What should always be added to the 'no pain, no gain' approach is the thought: 'given that you wish to stop with the modern approach'. The modern idea of action encourages us to view 'gain' as inherent to the active process. It is considered necessary that the active principle and the gained substance be somehow seen as involved in a mechanical cause and effect relationship where the act brings about the otherwise totally inert effect. When we act, so it is thought, we stimulate something into life which otherwise does not even come into consideration for life. Pain is accurately enough accepted as something that should not regulate or rule any further action, but that is as far as it goes. An intelligent interpretation of pain as something that a., does not need to play a role, and b., can be creatively suffered, is not part of this modern approach to life. This is also why it must always remain an approach. Modern man catches as much as a glimpse of the promised land but he cannot enter. The glimpse, periodically, keeps him going and at best on his toes, but in order to arrive at life and actually live it he has to lay down his modernity. Human beings have to realize that it is their fate to give meaning and substance to all other beings, and that they are destined to derive meaning and substance themselves from their relationship with all beings. There is the creative relationship and then there is the merciful outpouring.

So it comes as no surprise that the step, or transition, from our perception of beings to our endowment of beings – or from our accumulation of conscious reality, in this present case of the element of accumulation (the cumulative element), to the actual enjoyment of life – involves no pain. To put it another way, to get from one to the other we need not die. It is, after all, not a case of getting from a former to a latter. There is really no such thing as a step or a transition, for that which is gained is contemporary to that which is done in order to gain it.

So even as we understand (perceive) the cumulative element, so does the life accumulate for us. It is, of course, life in a specific mode, namely conscious reality in this case. When we look at it directly it appears as the <u>realm</u> of conscious reality which we mentioned earlier, which realm is the condition for the life which does not fail. As soon as we concentrate our perceptive faculty once again on the being in question, in our present case on the cumulative element, the conscious reality as life accumulation comes into its own again.

So much depends here on actually doing what we talk about while we talk about it. It never works out to the satisfaction of anyone if the topic under discussion is held at arm's length. More is involved here than a topic, and certainly discussion is not the essence of what we do.

What usually stands in the way of a perfect communication in these matters is our insistence, somehow, on sensation. We demand sensation, either disingenuously as evidence for what we suppose depends on us for judgment, or rationally and logically as the necessary precursor for understanding. The former objection sounds like this: "How do I know you are not lying if you cannot offer me a sense experience?" and the latter sounds like this: "How can I understand what you mean, if you give me nothing for my senses?" All the same, no sign is given. If a sign were forthcoming, we would, in fact, do well to ignore it.

The life accumulates where none may see it. This we must say in response to the question: 'Where?' if it did accumulate here or there we could not be sure of it. But equally in response to the question "Where?" we must respond, more positively: "Wherever we choose to live."

The choice of life over death is not a self-evident one. Not that anyone ever consciously says: "I choose death", but the multitudes choose it all the same, though they call it life.

Through perception of the cumulative element we accumulate life where we may choose it instead of death. This free choice of eternal life at any given time amounts to a marvellous power, for we may literally overcome death as we see fit. By death we mean anything that overcomes our organs, our faculties and finally ourselves. We may notice the beginnings of this and act right away. What we have accumulated stands us in good stead now. We may notice a darkening of the conscious realm of reality, and right away we may choose life, we may access that pool of vitality which is nowhere to be found except for the purpose of once again overcoming some particular death – of our organs, our functions or ourselves.

Care must be taken not to be waylaid by a sensation or a sign. This above all is important, that neither the accumulation of life nor the accessing (birth) of new life is considered to be sensible or sensational. We must train ourselves to know from faith and to understand from faith in this case. Elements are percepts of faith. First we must look to our faith, (which has nothing to do with Christianity or with any other religion but with our fundamental human faculty) and then we can operate in terms of it, on the basis of it and in line with it. Actual sensation then begins where faith has become sufficiently operational.

The cumulative element is the one we do well to keep in mind whenever we search or do research for life. Human beings exist right close up to the source and origin of life and all other beings really depend on them to make use of this privilege. The way we relate to other beings, all of which participate in humanity (humanity being the essence of being) either augments or diminishes us, so we do well to invest some time in reflections on this topic. The best we can do, usually, is to interpret what occurs to us as we contemplate the beings that we have singled out for attention. Perception, however, improves on this because perception is always to some extent elementary. While we do it we know that we do it and at the same time we know what goes on even though we have no sensible evidence of it. We know that what goes on is truly worthwhile, and we acknowledge that unless we are aware of it going on, it cannot go on for us in such a way that we have the benefit of it right here and now, not after pain and death.

This whole business of an accumulation of life makes sense only, of course, to those who know that one of their tasks as human beings is the practical transfer of life. Those who are not committed to this will not even understand what is meant here by life. They will not know what is meant by the giving of one's life. Nowadays we have to make some fairly elaborate decisions if we want to counteract the modern paralysis of spirit and being. We have to be willing to step right out of the modern systems of thought and patterns of feeling, clogged as they are by half-heartedness and falsified by presumption, before we can take advantage of a few simple benefits that accrue not on account of what we suffer or do but because we are beings that have what it takes to be human. Our natural rank is the thing that puts us in mind of these benefits in the first place. Of course if we would rather sleep or be dead, no one can make us wake up and live, at least not if we insist on it. So we either take matters in hand and mature or we do not and remain immature, a burden to those around us.

What we have described here as the cumulative element is simply such a way of taking matters in hand. There is really no advantage to dissent or argument on these matters. We either take hold or turn elsewhere.

(27/1/'96)

17

Spiritual Perception

That we should be able to look at one another and at the world around us and see what delights us, this is one thing, and many of us wish we had the knack of it, for mostly we only see things that depress us, falsehood and lies. But then we would wish to see beyond what delights us, for if we stop with that, it cannot compete with an urgency in ourselves that soon clouds our eye, so that once again we stare back at misery and all is despair. We would learn how to look beyond what delights us, and in order to do that we must call on our spirit, for our eye in itself lacks sufficiency.

So there we create for ourselves an image of the world that coincides with our spirit. We become our spirit for a time of work. This is marvellous work. We become that spirit and we let it take us where it would, but we remain superbly alert. This spirit of ours is the same as the one that exits without us, and differs from that only in that it exists within us and is available to us for work.

Now we might say we are free to do this spiritual work, but really we are only at liberty to do it, and we cannot be free, technically, until we do it. Once we have done it we are at liberty again.

105

At liberty, we may choose freedom, but we are also at the mercy of various deleterious influences and liable to setbacks, so the sooner we choose work towards freedom the better.

Spiritual perception is such work. We become one with our spirit and undergo change. How do we become one with our spirit? We know that we have a spirit. Our spirit is a gift from the one who is good spirit. In personal terms, he has given part of himself to us. He who is immense in himself has moved into us and has thereby become a measure or part of himself. I am expressing this as well as it can be expressed.

First we must come to terms with the fact that we, as human beings, have such a spirit. And it won't do that someone has told us and we believe him. We must actually have sensed within ourselves the motion of this spirit. We must know that we have been moved by spirit and that we may therefore enlist our energies on behalf of it. We know that this spirit is good because it is peaceful. If it were to excite and to arouse us and to give us a sense of power it would not be good and we would admit that we were on the wrong track. Good spirit always is peaceful and never presumptuous.

So we look for this peaceful good spirit within ourselves and we enlist our energies on behalf of it until those energies are quite swallowed up by it. This is the first stage on the road to spiritual perception. It has to do entirely with what goes on within ourselves. We identify our energies, all the impulses that tend to bring us into focus and all the stimulants that cause us to lean in a certain direction and we allow these to be embraced by the good spirit of whose presence in ourselves we have first-hand knowledge. And remember that in the absence of such first-hand knowledge we will not be able to cope because either our energies will engulf us, because we mistake them for good spirit, or else we will mishandle them as mechanisms, towards spurious goals. Our firsthand knowledge of good spirit is of the essence and crucial.

As soon as no energy is left in us we can say that we have become one with our spirit, and now spiritual perception may begin. We may begin to perceive spiritually. How do we go about this? We simply wish to do it and already we do it. Anyone who is one with his spirit only needs to wish to do something and he is doing it. It goes without saying that while we are one with our spirit we are only able to wish to do what is good for us to do at that moment and at that time.

So we wish to perceive spiritually and we perceive spiritually. But what do we perceive? Once again, we may perceive what we wish. We are one with our spirit and consequently only beings can occur to us, not things. Beings are created. We may perceive whatever being or beings we wish to perceive.

And what might be our reason for such spiritual perception? We do not do it for its own sake, or because it gives us pleasure, though it may do. We do it because it reveals to us our working relationship with whatever being or beings we perceive. And the revelation of such relationships means that we may enter into them.

So the second stage has to do with the revelation of a working relationship between ourselves and a being, and it begins by our wishing to perceive and continues by our choosing to perceive beings or a being. The choice we make is not different from the wish to perceive that particular being. And the working relationship is revealed to us as a deepening and as a strengthening of our certainty about that being.

Next we have to ask how we go about stepping into that working relationship. We notice how the being we perceive becomes increasingly more vivid to us. We are much more certainly aware of its presence. And we acknowledge readily that not only that being becomes somehow more powerfully alive, but we do too. There is an intimacy about such a relationship – or perhaps we should say: about this relationship – that makes us wish we could prolong the experience, perhaps render it permanent. But unless we step into the relationship itself, it only serves to remind us of what might be and of what has been. The relationship in all its luminous vibrancy is revealed – then concealed. We feel cheated – bereft – disappointed. We know now Tantalus must have felt.

This third stage, of stepping into the working relationship that stands revealed to us, is the most crucial in our time because we are least familiar with it. We have for so long confused being alive with really living that upon the revelation we sit back and – taste despair. Then we hasten to repeat the experience. Being alive, however, is being on the road to having life. While we are alive we move towards life. An important fact needs to be rehearsed here, and it has to do with our readiness for action. So far we have wished to be one with our spirit and we have wished to perceive a being or beings, and we have known in our heart that as we wished so we fared. As we believed so it became us. Now something additional is required, for which we may not have the patience or the stamina, since each time it presents to us something unfamiliar and new, something towards which we must move with our own entire being. We must move towards it, not just lean towards it, and we must move with our entire being, not merely with our perception, our will, our intellect and such like. I does not suffice that we wish to move but we must actually move. What this means has to be carefully thought about, since it in itself may come to us as a wonderful revelation.

You are one with your spirit and perceiving the being you wish to perceive when suddenly the relationship between you and it comes alive. There is a moment of indecision. You are ready more or less to marvel, to worship even. But you have many times in the past experienced how short-lived this experience is, especially when you attempt to grasp the pleasure of it. As soon as you move towards the experience it leaves you in the lurch. Is it not as if you were grasping something for yourself when really the relationship concerns not only you but both you and the being or beings you perceive? Is it not as if, by moving towards the experience of the revealed relationship you were in a sense betraying the being you had perceived? By perceiving a being you are saying to that being: "You and I are related and I wish to bring that to our attention so that ... both of us may benefit." Then suddenly you make as if to take all the benefit onto yourself. No wonder things go wrong. No wonder the love affair turns sour. Next time try something else. As soon as the relationship is perceptively revealed to you, concern yourself entirely with the being the perception of which, or of whom, resides in you now. What you have perceived is with you, you may take that for granted. Now what about the being the perception of which resides in you? You have changed a little, due to your perception, and this is good. Now what about investing your small change in the perceived being? Let the revelation of the relationship, which convinces you so much of your aliveness, stand as a reminder and work as a transition. We call it a working relationship precisely because something is at work here. But as yet this work is only potentially, not actually of benefit to you. The transcendence that is to extend your small change into a major change has yet to come about – to be brought about.

The only way you can step into that revealed working relationship is – by making that being your own. You have perceived a being, you have discovered your working relationship with it; now make that being your own. This is an act of love. You take more of an interest in that being than in yourself while at the same time you remain, of course, perceptive. The ongoing perception is of the utmost importance, otherwise you begin to interfere with that other being and you mistake your interference for good doing.

The perceptive interest in and concern for that other being now will be productive of life for you, and you may take that for granted. By choice you have transcended your own individuality and adopted, assumed, or even accepted the being of another being, specifically of the being you perceive.

It sounds a bit far fetched, to speak of the being of a being. Our imagination would seem to break on that rock. But while you are an entity, existing in your own right, you also participate in the same act of creation as all beings. You are created, but you are also creative. Being created, you are unique. All beings are unique, not only human beings. Each and every act of creation is productive of a unique individual being, though we may not right away be able to reach for the appropriate definition. But being created, you are also in your turn creative, like all beings – unless of course you have neglected that creativity, which is possible only for human beings. And we may say that all beings are equally creative of life. This is so, whether we have any evidence of it at just this moment or not. Human beings have a special status and therefore they may fall short in their creativity. They may even become totally uncreative, espousing popularity and turning into changeless mass beings. Then they themselves find themselves sociologically interesting! But that is another matter. The point to ponder here is that all beings, human beings included, are productive of life in terms of that working relationship that has been revealed to us and into which we step inasmuch as we perceptively take upon ourselves that other being's creativity or being. We take it upon ourselves, we allow for it and make room for it in ourselves. We let that other being tell us about itself, to put it more metaphorically.

Our language seems ill equipped to deal with this aspect of human action, but this has to do with custom and usage. The metaphors of today are the concepts of tomorrow, and vice versa. The modern fallacy is to fall back on revelation rather than to transcend with it. We have called the relationship that is revealed due to perception of beings a working relationship precisely in anticipation of this need to transcend, to 'climb across', before we can have actual life rather than merely being alive for a time. It should be enough to call it a relationship, but not many of us are used to relating dynamically. We have come to think of relationships as static conferences of meaning which merrily transpire and then of course expire, quite independently of whether we do or do not.

So we need to emphasize that this final transcendence both resides ambitiously in the relationship and must be instituted by us by way of a creative act. It is no good pretending it will all be done for us, nor should we presume to be able to do it ourselves alone. The pretension and the presumption are both modern, which implies a falling back, short of the goal, into a sham reality or an overreaching of oneself, wide of the goal, and ending up with a false reality.

Spiritual perception is required right up to the point of the creative act, where we take upon ourselves the being of the being we perceive. This creative act, this act of love, is always and again a renewed output of power by ourselves. We tend to shrink before the power of the being we perceive, or we tend to overpower it, so we miss out on life. Only in cooperation with the revealed (working) relationship can we gain our end, and only due to (spiritual) perception can the relationship be revealed to us. If we initially do not become one with our spirit, or if we suppose we have no spirit, we cannot even begin to perceive, and what we will then call perception is a mere judgment according to appearances and an uninformed manipulation of data.

————————   (3/2/'96)

18

Spiritual Perception and Education

To own our spirit, this implies a readiness for work, and really it means work. Nothing exemplifies so promptly our human/divine power as creative action. The example we set in this way is crucial both for the young and for the immature. As we work, so we change. This change, in the case of us human beings, can be described as the taking upon ourselves, or the suffering, of other being, so that our own being does not degenerate.

Very well, you say that you are, but do you know that you are and do you have any evidence of it? The only evidence that you can really have of it is due to your overcoming of moments, intervals and periods of degeneration. We can even speak of the modern times as a time of degeneration. And of course this degeneration is to be seen relative to demands made and goals set by reality itself. If we degenerate we do so in view of the creative reality that 'is the case' however we feel, think or behave.

And while the degeneration amounts to our neglect or usurpation of creative reality, to the point perhaps, where we are not even any more aware that there is such a thing, so does the overcoming of, or the cessation from, such degeneration imply our espousal of real spirit. We must be able to say: "Yes, I wish to be real; I desire to be worthy of this real spirit so that it may move in me, and I would like to be empowered by this spirit so that I may act in cooperation with it. I accept that my hands must be clean, my head clear and my heart uncluttered if humanity is to be my lot and not popularity my liability, so I am willing to take pains to achieve those three goals."

But how to go about this. Chastity, humility and discipline sound like echoes from a by-gone age. Today we have something on the cards called education. We are to be pulled out, extracted from our degeneration, and those who are to make this possible and more possible, for us are to be mature human beings with clean hands, clear heads and uncluttered hearts.

We can make an interesting comparison between education and pedagogics. Education implies a withdrawal and a liberation from, which is to say, presumably, from conditions and states of degeneration. Pedagogics on the other hand suggests a guidance. Now children, as we know, are in need of guidance towards maturity and freedom, but they must also be drawn out of various unfortunate habits and tendencies which obstruct their natural growth. If we like we can regard education and pedagogics as both sides of the same coin, and certainly no one can be liberated if he is not at the same time guided. The guiding and the liberating must go hand in hand. Both must be involved in our mature attitude and approach to the young and the immature, whether the word education or the word pedagogics is just fashionable in our present time.

At the same time we must keep in mind that children have it as part of their physical being to be urged towards maturity – while they cannot achieve this maturity, or come to it, entirely from within themselves and on their own. They require mature examples. Simplified, children want to grow up and they must have maturity held out to them.

Now spiritual perception is definitely a function of maturity. Not only an adult is require for it, but it must be a mature adult. It should suffice to speak of perception, but I emphasize the point by calling it spiritual perception in order to accommodate those who mistake the detached processing of dead data for perception. Spirit and reality go hand in hand, so we could also call it real perception.

Imagine now a teacher who is capable of real perception. He will perceive these young beings, his pupils, and he will perceive other beings; and he will perceive all these beings in a working relationship. He will be aware of the hidden dynamic link between all these beings, himself included, and he will know how his continued and repeated perception serves to make that connection more and more obvious. He considers it very much worthwhile that his connectedness and the exchange of humanity implied by it should be drawn to everyone's attention. We will leave to one side for the moment what his reason is.

He knows, this teacher, that his spiritual perception alone suffices to bring out into the open the relationship of all the beings he perceives. This is an immensely important thing for him to know, and he will have to remind himself of it frequently. In the absence of ongoing perception his task, and all his tasks, are doomed to failure. They do not even get off the ground. His indispensible maturity and his being one with his spirit are really one and the same thing. His perception must be based on these.

And then of course very gradually the various working relationships between these beings which he chooses to perceive arise and are revealed to him. He changes. He behaves, he speaks: he acts. One thing leads to the other. We cannot become aware of a working relationship and not express our joy, our pleasure: our satisfaction. The teacher does this. He becomes an example of human maturity. This exemplary being of his has its roots in a natural spontaneity which may be traced to working relationships, if we wish to know how it starts and where it begins, but of much greater interest to the teacher in action will be the forming and shaping of this naturally spontaneous exemplary being.

Out of his ongoing relationship with the child he teaches will arise the particular forms and shapes he seeks. "How will I go ahead now and express my motivation in the presence of this pupil and for the benefit of this pupil?" he asks himself.

And the answer must come to him as the final fruit of his spiritual perception of the child and of related beings. It might begin with an answer to the question: "What am I to say?" – or to the question: "How am I to behave and what shall we do together, this pupil and I?" Really there is no need to assess the pupil, outside any working relationship, because such assessments will only clutter the teacher's heart. He does not stand back from the child and make judgments, appraisals and diagnoses on which he then bases later behaviour or approaches to the child. He treats every child on the basis of a present interrelationship, and this includes even how he thinks and feels and talks about that child to others, because at such times he must be very careful not to talk or behave as though he were not in reality in a working relationship with that pupil. Memory must serve him perceptively, in other words.

How we are and what we do inwardly must always come first. A teacher must every time be prepared in head, heart and hand before he approaches a pupil or pupils. Perception as such has no part in this because perception is outward, of beings, not inward, of being.

The preparation of the teacher prior to perception is of his being. He can enter upon such preparation both by himself and with others. Although he does not perceive yet, he is being perceptive, and in the three ways mentioned above: head, heart and hand.

Perceptivity of the head has to do with clarity achieved or matters to do with self, psyche and society, so that he learns to differentiate between these and himself, his soul and his community. In these pages we can only give an outline. Discussion of such matters is not enough. Actual training has to be undertaken, practices and habits have to be learned and acquired.

Perceptivity of the heart falls into two categories, namely those of love and affection. The teacher cannot hope to succeed with his pupil if he muddles these two. Affection is human-natural and may be sustained in the interest of trust and closeness, while love participates in reality and is merciful.

As for perceptivity of the hand, here the teacher must examine and come to terms with his motivations and reasons for doing what he does. Is he essentially isolated from his pupils and forever out to win them over to his side? Is he forcing them into a pattern so that he can have his own way? Is he looking for gratitude? For pleasure? For sacrifice? Or perhaps for ideal or standard results? Clean hands means upright motivations and a healthy respect for the rights and the individuality of others, especially if we have chosen to be responsible for their welfare.

The outlandish attitude some so-called teachers have towards their charges forever forces them into a defensive position. Every 'lesson' is an elaborate impropriety and children hasten to rid themselves of this burden by developing a callous indifference.

If we try to imagine a teacher without even this perceptiveness, we are bound to fail utterly. If we do not perceive our own being, however can we be of use to others on their way to maturity and freedom? If we have not yet found our own way to our inwardness we cannot possibly have any useful outward effect. As for that initial road inward, there are no shortcuts, no mechanic advances, no organic tricks. And it matters a great deal what and how we believe. Anyone whose outlook on the world remains, in the main, wilful or intellectual will find himself fighting an endless battle. The trials he undergoes will seem meaningless to him. So with the endless trials of the unperceptive teacher. Forever he in turn criticizes or sickens and becomes a trial to his charges. He must begin from at least one of these three positions of head, heart and hand, and penetrate to the core of his human being. Let his thoughts become ruled by an intelligence that surveys the world not as a finite arena of competition or as a place of endless indulgence but as unlimited creation of particular significance. Such a stance will discipline his thought, not in any particular direction at first, but more in the service of genuine thought itself. We may ask for such an intelligence; we may simply long for it and it arrives. But if this casts too much of a shadow for us, we might attempt entry by way of our heart. Here it can help immeasurably to be mindful of the fact that we cannot be good. Not we ourselves can be good, and yet there exists within us an appetite for goodness. The resulting tension, so long as we can sustain it, is profitable.

If neither by head nor by heart he makes inroads, then let him be active in terms of his utmost ambition, but in such a way that success and failure are equally meaningful to him, in the light of something else, namely the drive to exist, to be around, to be persuasive and influential. There is something in each one of us that asserts itself and urges us to do. We go astray here only to the extent that we remain unaware or become ignorant of this urge. Then it becomes inadvertently linked to false goals and petty ambitions and little pleasures. In some of us this urge to do is stronger than in others, so that in our case this may be the narrow gate through which we enter into perceptiveness of our being.

Here all is well ordered and perfectly reliable. We do well to let those who know inform us that our own being, whatever else we are, is well ordered and reliable. Naturally we cannot have any evidence of this until we have entered, so frequently it happens that we shy back as if we feared insanity or as though we were about to do something illegal. Without courage and trust we get nowhere. A teacher would look for a master. Perceptive of his being he will know his master. The one he seeks has long been enshrined here, but unable to do more than assist him in secret. It suffices for us even to be intentionally perceptive, intending to perceive our own being, for this assistance to become evident to our being. This is remarkable, because our senses are not involved, and yet we have a consciousness of being. We intend to be perceptive and right away there is a consciousness of the helpful hand. That same hand seems to withdraw as we cease in our intention. Once again we make clear our intention to perceive our being and there right away the assistant meaning offers to teach us, to show us how to advance and develop in perceptiveness. Diligence is of the essence. Only those who are in earnest need apply for final results. Does it seem to them then perhaps a little presumptuous to call themselves teachers when they realize how much they themselves stand in need of being taught?

Once we have become sufficiently perceptive of our own being, we will almost automatically demonstrate an ability to perceive beings, and then we will wish to let others share in our benefit. What a horror, to observe those who are not perceptive,

117

who are not even endowed with a notion of such a thing as their own being, as they undertake to instruct others in the ways and means of nature and reality, of beauty and truth! They call themselves teachers and have nothing to offer but the trap of their impotence, the trick of their blindness.

_____

(5/2/'96)

19

World-Building

The New Jerusalem – the new world: with every fibre of our being we build on it. As if we could do different! It horrifies us, to imagine that we might do otherwise.

Perceptive of our being, perceiving other beings, we daily bring to a conclusion in our works, by way of our work, the creative beginning and middle of ourselves. How could we possibly come to terms with the world of things, with the world we can point at, if we did not perceive it as the world of beings in reality? Everything, this chair, this loaf of bread, this person next to me, may no longer be merely significant to me, but here we are called upon, each hour of every day, as responsible human beings, to reveal how they share in our being and how we do in theirs.

Truly when something occurs to us as a thing, this is the invitation of a being that we should quickly come to know it. Sufficient perception is all that is missing, and then the creative act. We are at fault because we believe that eternal life feeds on the future.

But either we are stumped in our attempt to express the errors of our times while we live in splendour, or else we delineate these errors correctly, with style, while reality perplexes us. Indeed we may choose. All has been accomplished, insofar as our human reality is concerned, that cannot be accomplished by us. The rest is entirely up to us. This is truly good news, and exceptional cause for certainty. Such freedom it gives us, to be able

118

to say: "If my life seems miserable, this is no fault of my life but of me." In our hands rests the welfare ordained by our god.

So if it comes down to that, we are cut out to be builders. We have the plans, the knowhow and the strength. Nothing is missing except our daily, our hourly, getting-down-to-it. We have mistaken the cause of our fatigue, of our ignorance, of our lack of example. It begins with death. Unless I know it as a thing of which the significance has been stripped, I am bound by its significance. How much effort shall I then invest in this knowledge? Why, simply a sufficiency. Do we not climb a mountain because we wish to get to the top? Is it the fault of the mountain if we stop early? Shall we in future define mountains with their peaks halfway up?

Perhaps in our present times we should, instead of death, say pain. It should be confessed that death, far from binding us with its mistaken significance, has not even that significance. One would have to upgrade it, as some poets have done, to return it to that mistaken state, so that we might understand that its significance has been stripped from it.

Better to speak of pain. As pain, death is at least sensually present, so how can we fool ourselves. There is always some pain for anyone who is alive. Only the dead believe in painlessness. As soon as life announces itself as pain they kill it. Better to be dead than in pain.

A difficult proposition. I too would rather be dead if I imagined that pain were devoid of significance. Is it not bad enough that we have lost, or not gained yet, the ability to suffer?

But what does that mean? Who can help me out? Do I suffer at this moment? Most decidedly. I state categorically before the world that at this moment I suffer. I support the pressure at present of this creative task in hand. And did you suppose that I glowered above it after the manner of an intellect? I assure you I suffer. It is being brought home to me painfully, the necessity of this task, and gladly I submit. Let me go further than that. I submit with a definite and passionate excitement which I must keep in check lest it spoil my voice.

Am I ready to suffer the barrenness between creation and creation? Most assuredly, being entirely at liberty to see through my mistaken notion of it as a barrenness. Shall there forever be a panic between intake and outlet of breath? Shall there forever be a frantic exertion prior to the beginning of every new breath taken? Or shall we instead resign ourselves to the enlivening rhythms of our suffering? A courageous resignation to sense is required after intervals of madness.

Not until we sense the reason for pain, the precious purpose of it, do we no longer need it. But until then, if we mean to live, we do need it.

It seems plausible that we lost all sense of that purpose through sheer neglect. However, not only that. Not only did we neglect to build the new world, which was bad enough, because it cost us our reason, but we built instead, and often how frantically, a substitute world of things, which cost us our life. Now we should think that over. Perhaps our hands are clean enough at the moment and we can try something fresh. But not while we look to our thing-oriented minds to guide us painlessly to Elysian fields. First we shall need to say Yes to the pressure, to the depression, to the grief and to the misery, indeed to everything unfortunate that besets us – and at the same time a vigorous No to those energetic muscle spasms that tempt us into popular action. Avoid every impulse of bravado, of overweening high spirits, of victory and triumph in the eyes of others, otherwise how can you be sure of your dismay and of your despair? If you mask your pain or if you pretend you have none (because only the healthy and good man has justification of life!) then how can you suffer? And if you cannot suffer, how shall you live?

If you cannot suffer, how shall you work, indeed; be more honest and consequent. Not that your suffering is itself a fine work. The plans are delivered, the bricks have arrived, the men stand waiting. No, you swear it concerns someone else. Another points out your mistake to you, you blame him too. You will not allow these materials and means and capacities to be delivered onto you. Oh, if you had set your sights in preparation, how could you mistake these deliveries, in short, this deliverance? If only you had taken the promise and the warning to heart! You should never have mistaken the gift for a curse, the greeting for an insult.

But why moan about it? Take the promise and the warning to heart now.

Half through with this talk I feel elated and at peace. Even these are materials, these feelings, that shall go into the building. So in a deep sense I must suffer my feelings of joy and satisfaction. The workmen are smiling, the plans are clear, the weather is fine. Time to down tools and stretch out on the grass? A recipe for disaster. The new world is built in fair weather and foul. We need more craftsmen, who recognize their guilt and their shame, their horror of themselves and their terror of these times, as raw-materials pure and simple; who will not get drunk when the master is away but persevere alike in happiness and good health; who will not beat the one who is sent to return them to their task but will suffer the outrage, the injustice, the indignation, indeed as if they had deserved them. It helps to pretend here. Before the pressures of the new life, since I know I cannot be in the right, and since I am all too quick to insist I am nonetheless in the right, let me for the time being pretend I am in the wrong. Then, later, half blessed with insight, I shall know with a certainty, and gladly, that I was wrong.

Such are the skills of the planners, who must know the ground to serve as foundation. The type of my individuality is the book I must study if all is to go well. In one way I have made a thousand mistakes, so it might be best to avoid that way altogether. In another way I have made only a hundred, so here I harbour hope of correction. Pain never ceases to frighten me, so why not make sense of that fear? Then I like to indulge myself in mockery, to luxuriate in cynicism, to take my leisure in criticism. But I think I know a way of serving these up for the letter to kill, so that the spirit may live. Then it settles on me like a plague that there is nothing left to do. All has been settled. Have I not said it all? I should only repeat myself. Oh delicious boredom! Such vanity in boredom! But wait a moment. I have at my disposal – I as a human being – the key to the workshop of final creativity. What am I doing with it? Here, sit down with me now and help me puzzle this out. The spectre of nihilism sits perched on my shoulder, in tears for the lack of a project. My heart goes out to him. I show him my ego, my self. Quickly he takes possession and rushes down the hillside, into the water.

We do much more sometimes by waiting. It goes on within us then, with a graded purpose of its own. All we need to come up with is a little intelligent trust. If we cannot construct, with our customary alacrity, why, perhaps it desires for the moment to give shape to itself. Sometimes the best we can do is just supply the stage, for the plan to be able to go on. Or we lend our faculties, passively, to the fact that the new world 'is'. Certainly we should need no such guarantee of our worthiness as energy pulsing through our veins. Outwardly we may well look like death warmed over, but within us a silent awareness disports itself, while we know that and tolerate. Why should it be absolutely crucial that we understand everything that goes on and is done on our behalf? Perhaps all that is needed is that we should let it happen. There are such events. Not that we lack the wits to compare it, but the nerves to bear it. Gratitude, not jealousy is the order of the day.

What, then, are the ideal conditions for work on the world? In truth, there are none. Once we have swallowed this bitter pill we are finally on the way to a human maturity of sorts. Until then we fumble among dust and abstracts. The only condition worth its salt is our human condition, which is life in the light of day on earth. Behold, you are born, now sign on the dotted line. You hesitate? There lies your original sin, quivering in front of you. All else that inhibits the hand of your creator on our behalf now originates in that initial hesitation – and may be removed as soon as we intend to make it good. Unless we accept it, the gift of existence can never be crowned by the gift of life. No fealty of kinship is extended to the reluctant servant, to the rebellious slave. Until we bless our present state we deserve no better. Those who build the new world do not change the world, they change in themselves. They are so open to change, as they mingle their being with the being of others, that their change becomes constant. At their whirring centre time has stood still and space has become limitless, while rest is utterly the cause of their intrepid action. They perceive other beings, from the great spiral of creation, and on behalf of the relationship they leap into action, first voluntarily, overcoming each time their impatience or distaste, and then gradually much more with spontaneous good habit. Wise intention takes root in faithful spontaneity. After this manner again and again, in many departments, from youth to old age, until the time has arrived for that final spontaneous lap, when those around us acknowledge with satisfaction that the smile on our lips is not for them only.

How we perceive the world and one another today depends to some extent on how we perceived them yesterday, and whether or not we perceived them at all. Let us at least be perceptive of our own being, for we transport the makings of the new world about in ourselves. Who shall pity us if we do it unconsciously? If sleep overcomes us while yet there is light, we merely add fuel, at best sensationally, to the modern tragedy, of which few are persuaded. When the materials are used up, it may be time to transcend. Really the new world is linkage revealed from being to being, all due to our human personal transcendence, at the moment of ripeness, perhaps when all else has failed. There is a momentary stillness, then a rush to the end, or a glimpse of surpassing beauty. You cannot yet live in it, until the last stone is in place, the one rejected by the builders.

_____

(8/2/'96)

20

What is Perception?

Perception is a knowledgeable approach towards outward, not inward reality, and it is not any approach to what lies outside us. Sensation distinguishes between what lies outside us and outward reality, but shows us both on an imaginary common basis. This common basis of outward reality and outside things is an illusion, and a helpful one, because we need to become somewhat adept at sensation before we can perceive. Our sense organs, foremost our eyes and ears and the sense of touch, tell us: "This is a thing, it exists somehow outside of us, on the other side of a partition, a curtain, a veil, as it were," and then: "This is not a thing but something else, a something that leaves me free of that excitement I feel in the presence of things outside, and I sense almost a kinship, a closeness of origin and purpose." Both have about them a sensible quality, something that stirs my body or promises to satisfy it. Sensation is bodily, so both these things and that something are experienced as being endowed with bodies. If they were not, how could we possibly sense them?

The source of excitement and the source of satisfaction are imagined to be of the same stamp while sensation has developed for us sufficiently to let us notice that distinction, but prior to ay attempt at perception by us. We ignore blatant or bald sensation here, which is devoid of imagination and no credit to anyone.

As sensation continues to develop for us, we become increasingly curious with respect to this imaginary difference between that thing which stimulates us in some way and that source of reward which seems available to us at other times. We imagine more and more reasons and explanations for this difference, be-

124

cause we are not at all at ease with regard to this duality in our world. At times we are downright disturbed by it. The satisfaction is short-lived and appetite revives. The excitement in turn tires us and we end up bored. What we most resent, perhaps, is the accidental nature of both experiences. We would dearly like to control them, but all too often they master us. As soon as we opt for things alone, ignoring the other, we get a fresh sense of hope – which soon is dashed. There is energy, willpower and triumph, but then there is fatigue, weakness and failure. So we opt for the experience of leisure and contentment, we take it easy and mock the ambitious failures among us, the strivers after success. We know enough to do without this delusion of power. And then desire builds in us; we have hardly had time to congratulate ourselves on our superior wisdom. Imagination, and all the products of our imagination, are so important precisely because we need time for reflection, otherwise we would despair. In that sense imagination is a real blessing.

However our nature is such that we are not to stop at this state of imaginary union of something we sense, with temporary satisfaction, as not outside us and things we sense as excitingly outside us. However conciliatory our imagination and reflection become, with our best efforts, as we make use of myth and symbol, the old dichotomy reasserts itself as if to spur us on, and if we take umbrage it becomes a thorn in our side, so that we become resentful, cynical and critical.

We do well, therefore, to allow ourselves to be spurred on and to ask: "What is the next step? There must be more to reality than this eternal back and forth between the irrational fixation and the rational slumber, between religious fervour and mathematical uncertainty, indeed between a correctible truth and a terrifying beauty.

Only if we ask with sufficient persistence and with a perseverance that will not take no for an answer can we actually come out on the side of perception. So perception is born out of the discontent over the imaginary, 'but' somehow not quite real, synthesis or unification of two experiences: the experience of things, outside us, and the experience of something not outside us. Among us comes the stranger and urges: "What, do you not yet perceive?" we welcome him – or we reject him.

*

We have to leave things outside us alone when we opt for perception. The excitement, the energizing influence of that entire outside realm, has to be ignored for the time being, so that we can give our fullest possible attention to what we until now have sensed as being not outside us, but in some way related to us, in contact with us or influencing us. Now we notice that certain sensations that we might describe as inside us must also be ignored. The total complex of outside-inside sensation becomes more manifest as we commit ourselves not to it, but instead always and again to what happens within – and without us. The 'with' is the crucial experience. We are with the experience; it does not exist or go on separate from us, apparently quite independently of whether we exist or not.

Often perception takes off from a special experience that is described as deepening, strong, opening out, religious, mystical, especially beautiful and such like. Sometimes this is called a break-through, because for the first time sensation does not occur as on either one or the other side of a barrier or divide. Looking back, this is found disconcerting, in comparisons to the recent whole experience, in which we were included and to which we made a difference.

Not until the advent of perception do we discover that there is an inside to match the outside, both of which we must now shun, and that there is a without to go along with the within, both of which we now may take pains to espouse

*

The fact then is that we perceive sensations. Those within us have to do with our own being and those without us are of other beings. We can, now that we have begun to perceive, speak of our own being and of other beings. The sensations within us, due to perceptiveness, are, as it were, rounded off, so that we can now speak of our being, whereas previously we had only inward sensations. The same goes for those sensations without us, which are now, due to our perception, relevant to us as whole beings. We cannot sense our being, nor can we sense beings. Perception takes over from sensation now as our chief faculty, so that previously we knew, whereas now we understand what we knew then. Perception and understanding are one and the same.

To perceive a being means to grasp it in its full particularity, and this takes time. While we perceive, we know that we are making progress. We know that we accumulate something as time goes on. It takes us to remain aware of that if it is not to stop. This is probably the most difficult habit of all to form. Along with the being we must perceive the element of accumulation. We tend to get sidetracked by various sensations of progress, or inertia sets in. So again and again we have to return to this element of accumulation while we understand the being in hand.

But what is it that accumulates as a result of perception? It allows itself to be called wisdom. It is not absolute or abstract wisdom, but a wisdom that pertains properly to the being we continue to understand. If I perceive a certain human being, then the wisdom that accumulates has specific application to that human being, while at the same time increasing my faculty for perceiving other human beings and other beings. What I learn about you also has application for others.

Our perception of human beings is the most profitable, because he wisdom we gain applies to all other beings. But this perception is also the most difficult, because we have 'fallen out' with one another and usually find ourselves in the position where we have to make up for lost ground, which can be discouraging.

There is, however, one human being who has not 'fallen out' with us and who takes nothing amiss that we do, while at the same time he understands us perfectly. This human being is well worth getting to know. The wisdom we accumulate during the perception of him is precious. Hours of practice each day are really well advised. However we must do what we can, and admit that if we chose we could do more. There are times when nothing else seems worthwhile, and then we can still do this. If we grow tired, this is due to misapplication, for this perception vitalizes and revives. And this human being is with us always.

*

Our perception, or understanding, of the one human being who is not unrelated to us in anything is complete in the sense that we do not at the same time have to keep in mind that we are accumulating wisdom for this accumulation to proceed. We cannot ever have any sensation of him as a thing, of course, that exists outside or inside us. But it is possible to have a sensation of him as something within or without me, so that I may then perceive that sensation and understand him. As soon as we seek to understand him, as a matter of fact, we are furnished with a sensation of him – if we but knew. This sensation is not necessarily pleasant. What counts is our immediate perception of it in the light of the one whose presence we – believe. If we do not believe his presence, our perception of any sensation of him cannot really succeed because we are bound to mistake it, for a thing.

Now as soon as we believe his presence, rather than believing the presence of things, our perception of our own being (perceptiveness) and of other beings actually becomes easy because we do not any more have to struggle to stay clear of things inside and outside us, finally being free of them. However we may insist on hoping that such a one exists, and then of course we have a hard time of it.

Often the real difficulty seems to lie in our refusing to admit that it is up to us ourselves what we believe. We are, by nature, at liberty to believe as we choose – or, to bring it more down to earth, to believe as we dare. To believe prior to sensation, not subsequently, this seems to require an inordinate degree of courage. All the same, in most cases the struggle for perception has already been decided on the fundamental level of belief. Those who insist that they sense and that they believe what they sense are blinded by the subsequent need for perception. The light that can only be perceived must occur as impenetrable darkness to those whose sensation is not based on powerfully believing the one who emits and is that light.

So if we do not believe in the good spirit who is merciful love we are not properly capable of sensation, and if our sensation is wrong, perception cannot begin. The popular way, traditionally the broad highway, is to believe what we sense, and to take this for reality, and then to be dismayed when that reality is annihilated by the impenetrable darkness. The light that can only be perceived, not sensed alone, must occur to all on the face of the earth, whether popular or human. Now the human way, for those who choose it, is to fight for the power of belief that precedes sensation, so that neither stimulus nor affect has a hand in the making of it. This is traditionally called the narrow way, the strait gate or the path, because one at a time passes along or through, not a tribe, or a group, or a family, or a society. This power of belief is not something we must add on to ourselves, such as it would take to believe in ghosts, demons and myths, in systems and schemes, but it is of the nature of something we regain. It slumbers in us, perhaps we have forgotten or forsaken it, it has perhaps never been used. Only through use does this power of believing, of fundamental faith, actually come into being, which being is then human being and no longer popularity. In use this power is inexhaustible strength. When the light that can only be perceived begins to shine, we grow readily into perception. Since what we sense is beautiful, considering that what we believe is true, we are now able to perceive what is real.

In that way our perception of reality includes our sensation of the beautiful and involves our belief in truth. But if the root is not firm, the fruit is not forthcoming.

And note this: Perception is inseparable from action. sometimes e may have to return to our roots, to take hold more firmly, when all action and passion must be temporarily laid aside, and this will be difficult for us only in proportion to our dependence on unreal conception and behaviour. Such a return to our roots is then both curative and renewing, though it may seem like sickness and waste.

So the world of perception, not the world of sensation, is the one that lasts, the one 'without end', while the world of sensation 'ended', in both senses of the word, as soon as perception of reality became possible and fruitful.

_____   (10/2/'96)

21

Psyche and Soul

We do well not to use these two words interchangeably. With right do we speak of our soul, because we are either in the possession of it or else it makes no difference to us, so that, in the course of meaningful language, it makes no sense whatsoever to speak of 'the' soul. There is my soul, if I have one, and there is yours, if you have one. What that is, and what it amounts to, when we do have it, we shall look at in a moment.

First we need to acknowledge that it happens that we are not in the possession of our soul. This either happens at times, or it goes on for long periods of time. It is even possible that we permanently lose our soul.

At such times as when we are without our soul we are psychic. What it means, to be psychic, and what can only be described as being 'under the influence' of a psyche, or as 'being possessed' by psyche, can only be understood from the point of vantage of a working soul. Only a person with such a soul can help someone who is possessed by a psyche. The one who is possessed in this way does not always know it, nor does he always know that he needs help.

Psychology can therefore be practiced only from the level of a possessed or owned soul, while depth-psychology presupposes a soul on a high level. Depth and height have equal rights to qualification here. The loftier soul might rescue the more depressed psyche – myth works successfully within those boundaries.

To be psychic, to be under the influence of psyche, means first and foremost to be in a state of insufficiency. Complex longings are unsatisfied. Perplexing depressions remain unresolved. There is a harrowing back and forth between self-hatred and self-adulation, between fear and adoration of others and the world. Mood swings draw on seemingly unlimited resources of energy or a plague of indifference draws the pitiable individual into one illness after the other. The affective life is stimulated apparently for no other reason than that the carrier of it should experience betrayal. Spiritually not much is managed beyond a sporadic enthusiasm and degrees of visionary depletion.

A study of the psyche – and we can speak meaningfully of 'the' psyche – from the point of vantage of our soul is either historical or pointless. Such a study limits itself intentionally to a particular time, and knows its own setting, or else veers off into chaos, to seduce and to mislead. The comments in the previous paragraph in reference to the psyche apply specifically, therefore, to what we today experience when possessed by psyche. It would be uninformed and unwise of us to refer to the psyche as though it might exist independently from individuals of one sort or another. It possesses you or me, or someone else, otherwise there is no such thing. Its most frequent occurrences nowadays can charitably be talked about.

There is such a thing as an explanation, or reason, for the occurrence of psyche. Any psychic influence, or affect, is not merely accidental but significant. A psychic affect that reaches into our depth is profoundly significant. A coldly rational attitude would dismiss, even reject, the psyche or instances of it. This is not well done. On the other hand, a boldly irrational involvement would stimulate, intensify, even sublimate it, and this is ill done.

Either we participate in some form of rejection or sublimation of the psyche, or else we act on behalf of it, aware of the significance of its existence.

And what is the significance, in general, of psyche? That a soul is to be regained. In particular, 'a' psyche is the shadow of our soul, and we can arrive at our soul by interpreting the profile of this shadow. This would seem to be a suitably contemporary description.

Certainly we do well to keep our soul, and in our patience we possess it, so by all means be patient and avoid impatience. (What! Nowadays? – Precisely.) However, once you have lost your soul, it still exists, so do not despair. Let us together look at this thing you have instead, this psyche. It really helps if we do this together, because you on your own are tending to despair, I can tell. And even this despair is a psychic phenomenon. I shall think my own thoughts about it now, about this phenomenon, and I will say to you only the chosen words. Believe me, your psychic state has influenced, has affected me, and this is fine by me, for I know two things: one, I cannot help you back to our soul unless I have first-hand physical knowledge of your significant psyche, and two: I will gain in my own soul by helping you back to yours.

Your psyche, which the rationalist in me would fearfully reject and which the irrationalist in me would ambitiously manipulate – the human being in me would embrace lovingly. How dreadfully difficult for me to side with the human being in me! The agony and the ecstasy of the irrational seems so much more attractive. The might and the detachment of the rationalist seem so much more appealing. Back and forth I stray between these two, really under the influence of the same psyche that possesses you, getting to know it in detail after a measure and – after the flesh. For the time being we are both in the same boat, which leaks, while the storm builds. I must find my way through to the human being in me, and I will succeed as soon as my perception of the affective psyche vis-à-vis my owned soul and your potential soul gains significant ground.

The effective therapeutic handling of the psychic, and especially of the depth-psychic, state proceeds in terms of suffering. True psychotherapy is a case of suffering for another. If you wish to heal me of my psyche you must take my soulless state upon yourself, because only then will the healing word occur to you. It will not occur to you in reference to some recipe or method that leaves you separate and detached from me, nor will it occur to you if you too merely end up in pain and so we are both in pain and, drastically put, either die or kill each other.

If you would suffer on behalf of me in my psychic, soulless state, and if you would gain the due reward, it will not do for you to fall in with my pain or to argue and explain my pain away but you must suffer it. What does that mean? How can you do that?

A word, now, about my soul, when I do posses it. It operates as my soul, this is important to keep in mind, and there are such works which stem directly from my soul. But my soul occurs also on one hand as my body and on the other hand as my mind. Statically perceived, my mind and my body are face and obverse of my soul. Dynamically, there are the products of my mind, the fruits of my body and he works of my soul. My mind implies my soul and my body involves it. My body is the sum-total of all my available senses plus emotion, feeling and passion. My mind means thought, meditation and contemplation plus reflection. What a rich feast is my soul! What abundance of action and variety of behaviour!

How shall I choose now: soul or psyche?

But if I would possess my soul and its physicality in all its real concreteness, as a growing and mature human being, I cannot afford to rest on my laurels but I must with exceeding gladness suffer the pain of your psyche. Both the highest delirium and the lowest dejection of 'your' psyche cannot but cause me pain. Everything between these two extremes – cannot but cause me pain. How beneficial for both of us if I learn how to suffer!

Analysis can serve me. I need to examine how I shrink time and again from the single crucial act in the presence of your psychic state. But I must keep in mind that while no two souls are one and the same, all psychic states and all psyches are the same, are one and the same, inasmuch as they signal a greater power of soul. This is what chiefly should interest us about any psychic state or about any individual human being under psychic influence. There is no real cause to delve into dreams or to plumb the so-called sub-conscious. What could we possibly gain there? Superstitions and idols.

Every psychic state, if we but new it, heralds a greater power of soul. My soul casts a shadow because I have not yet faced up to an increase of light. Why would you argue with this shadow? Help me face up to the light, so that we both might see more clearly what appears in the new light.

Artists as such are never sufficiently consequent in relation to psychic phenomena. What we call artistry, in comparison to the art of the art worker, remains always to some extent, by connivance or choice, under the influence of the psyche, for money or fame. We stop being artists and becomes art workers as soon as we opt for concrete soul and for the suffering of psyche, on behalf of our fellow human beings.

But how can I suffer on your behalf what I sense you are going through in terms of psyche? Every fibre in me shrinks from the pain. This pain tends to dictate my action and to regulate my behaviour. Psyche is pain for the one who knows it as psyche, though the one who is possessed by it, sickened, made ill, maddened – may actually experience this as pleasure. There is an addiction to psyche, just as there is something like an anti-addiction to the rationalist rejection of psyche and to the irrationalist indulgence in psyche. The addiction and the anti-addiction – they feed on each other. What about the one, now, who would increase the power of his soul; is he fighting a losing battle? How can we suffer such a pain that is tied up even with the principle of pleasure? Surely this task is impossible.

It will have to be shown. If someone could be shown me who demonstrated such implicit trust in eternal human souls that he suffered even their collective psyche as it grew in proportion to his closeness to them, then I might myself come up with such trust, for I would be able to imitate and I would take courage from the fact that it had been done. If such a one existed now, or had existed in the past – or both – why then my task should be easier, since I would only have to learn to lean on him, especially when the pain gets worst and suffering most unlikely, as fear paralyses affections and hatred destroys the world.

But where should such a one have lived? And under what circumstances? Would the popular mind not falsify his memory and make a sham of his achievements? Would his tale not be told in terms so entirely psychic that a veritable psychology of him would have to be invented so as to rid these times of the false light obscuring the new light?

Best forget 'these times' and concentrate on our own time. Perhaps we have overlooked something – or someone. If we can see the thing that is required, how came we into the possession of that eyesight? Therein resides a mystery. Perhaps if we extend our trust on principle, not only where we feel, on evidence, that it is deserved?

The final relinquishment of the psychic ego can be terrifying. A few have managed it. We do well to look to them for guidance. They have suffered it through, with who knows whose help, that their psychic ego has been replaced by themselves in the realm of a whole soul.

_____

(3/3/'96)

22

The Constant Element

The way we behave under stress, or when things are not going our way and we feel unjustly done by, this is an indication of the degree of our constancy. Reasons may lie ready to hand in explanation for unsteadiness of purpose, but the point is that we cannot conceive of the road that lies ahead. All too often what we do in such cases is throw ourselves on the breast of opportunity or chance, as if we were persuaded that any movement at all must be an improvement on standing still. However, what we mean by standing still is more like the cessation of motion than anything else, so it seems understandable that we should opt for either unrest, or for its obverse, speed. He cessation of motion means death for us. A decision born out of the fear of death therefore lands us in speed or unrest, and both of these are decidedly detrimental. Unrest loosens our grasp on a meaningful existence while speed delivers us into the hands of an arbitrary fate. The twin fruit is insanity and catastrophe.

What we need, first of all, is a corrective factor. Speed and unrest do not shut out awareness, only consciousness. So we know, we notice, at the periphery of our attentiveness, that here we have once again slipped our moorings and we drift, rudderless and devoid of destination. Out of unrest come forth all the trivial inventions of the day which then turn into seeming necessities. We observe this and we wonder. Over the last two centuries we have drawn on unrest a great deal for our energy,

136

so that civilization has advanced a great deal and the West has become the envy of the East. From speed we draw our hope for instant advancement. We wish to be suddenly here or there, instantly at our goal, immediately accomplished, whether we make kitchen furniture, travel to New York or feel pleasure and think thoughts. The dream of instant advancement is brought on by speed in the first place, and then that dream dictates an even greater speed. Finally we assume that the approaching train must surely be on the other track, but alas!

The corrective in the face of speed or unrest is nothing more nor less than a moment of reflection. Our awareness of once again having gone out on a limb is really in itself such a moment, and all that matters is that we act on it. That moment of reflection allows us to take stock of our situation and – to experience remorse.

Even if we cannot at the time connect that experience to an sensible cause, we do well to acknowledge it. First we admit that it has come over us, that we did not engineer it. Then we recognize the choice to own or reject it. Then we do well to own it, even, I say, though we cannot in the world imagine just cause for it. Awareness gives rise to a moment of reflection, which in turn allows us an experience of remorse. I say 'allows', because decidedly we are the richer for it. Remorse enlists mind, body and soul, so that suddenly we are in an important sense connected, intact, where previously we were disjointed and frayed.

Our next step is, to make that remorse intentional. But intentional remorse is repentance. And here we have arrived at the element of constancy. We cannot sense it but it renders our repentance constant. Of course we may contemplate it in itself now, but not until our repentance ahs sufficiently proceeded. This is why repentance is so important because no other human faculty contains within it this element.

Intentional remorse is not a stronger sensation of remorse. Remorse itself is accidental, it comes over us. Therefore it is also accompanied by a sensation. There is more to it than that sensation. There is the spiritual cause of it, and what we must do now is be that spirit, while we ignore the sensation. The reason for the sensation is that our attention should be drawn to the spirit that informed us. The sensation of remorse is the herald of that spirit. As soon as we become that spirit, the remorse exists no longer and there is repentance, in the sense that we do it. The question is, how do we become a certain spirit?

Really we should ask, not how to become, but how to be a spirit, because the notion of becoming carries with it in our minds a change from one state or condition into another. But then we may equally have a misguided notion of being, when we suppose that being implies a lack of progress, whereas it simply means that the progress, instead of depending on action, may be taken for granted.

To be, or to become, then, spirit means wholly to rely on it and to know that you do so. It may help you to keep in mind that the spirit in this case of remorse is good. Bad spirit could not inform us with remorse; it would have to be something like levity or delight. I advisedly say: 'something like'.

Remorse happens to us. We are then able to intend, and this intention is a case of being or becoming the spirit that informed us with remorse. Then and there we have the element of constancy. How do we know that we have it? We have been told and we accept what we have been told. Why should we bother accepting this? Because doing so gains us a vital centre to our being. We may try to understand now what is meant by saying that this constant centre builds.

The repentance begins as we intend the remorse, but we may not right away be able to acknowledge the constant element. The process of repentance gradually abstracts all that stands in the way of that acknowledgment. There is no need to ask what it is that causes the difficulty, or how it got there. We are not in the business of confessing particular sins here, or of analysing our psyche. During this intentional process of repentance we become readily enough aware of all that which would interrupt the process. We take no time to look at whatever it might be that interrupts but we simply acknowledge that once again we have strayed and so we return to repentance, feeling remorse, first on account of having strayed. We can see here how good spirit helps us always by informing us with such remorse. It should also be plain what it amounts to if we become stiff-necked in the face of that remorse. It can happen that as soon as we feel remorse we reject the very idea of it, and this causes damage. It destroys and tears own our being. We are far too proud, inwardly, to admit that there might be any cause for remorse. We have spent so much time and effort justifying ourselves and we cannot bear it that this time should have been wasted. You might almost say that we have become incapable of remorse. The centre of our being, far from existing, has actually become in itself a destructive force, a black hole, so that to all intents and purposes we have become a danger to our environment and a snare to those next to us. Destructive forces issue out from us, and the worst of it is that those around us, who may not be particularly enlightened, experience these as exciting, as fascinating and flattering. Our being does not build but it cooperates in destruction and tends to scatter, to fragment, to pull apart. We have become remorseless, and incapable of remorse. Outwardly we may well seem successful and adjusted. Indeed modern culture and education has always aided and abetted this remorselessness. It has travelled under the banner of emancipation, of liberty and of enlightenment. Our situation is incredibly critical because literally good spirit cannot influence us. We have succeeded in becoming immune and impermeable to good spirit. At the same time we are like a rudderless ship on an endless elemental ocean. Often it happens that those who seem most free do in fact not even exist as human beings.

Remorse and sufficient repentance, however, brings us within reach of the constant element and here we may rest. Does it seem astonishing that at rest we should build? Character and integrity are being built. We have a centre to which we can relate our experience and from which we can draw a constant replenishment. But of course we must know what goes on. The constant element allows us to focus our creative strength, and then we become capable of doing many things in masterful fashion which previously only excited our ambition but after a time we fell away, defeated by circumstances or by our own shortcomings.

Character and integrity are built not only for ourselves but for what we do and accomplish. None of these elements make any sense except in terms of human beings in action and at work. Human beings as idle individuals do not exist. Which is also why a lack of centre shows up so painfully in a human being. Our very being itself is at stake. If we perpetrate a crime, we must know that we were not human beings and we come in for punishment essentially on that score. What we know as punishment under the law can only have this one real purpose, which is to create the condition of remorse, so that we may choose penitence and return to our human centre. The criminal who says: 'I wish I had not done it,' is not necessarily on the right track, because in addition he still needs to come to terms with *what* he should have been at the time, and with *who* he should have been, namely someone.

Remorse can disintegrate into self-pity. In that case we need to be careful how we advise the one who is caught in this trap. If we set him an example of repentance, this is better than any advice. The self-pity is bound to affect us. Our first response will probably be one of justifiable anger. From there we find our own way to remorse and then to repentance.

We feel remorse in relation to something we did, not because our performance fell below some general or social standard but because we could have done better. Remorse is therefore an indication to each one of us that under the circumstances we could have done better, not that we can be proven to have done wrong. Embarrassment on account of having fallen short of some social standard is therefore not remorse and it cannot serve as an opening to repentance. More often than not true remorse is not recognized but masked to look like something else. In order to understand why we might mask our remorse, we have to have a notion of what is at stake, namely our human being. Neglect of falsification of our human being results in true remorse, but not until we act on that remorse, repentantly, is our human being repaired or verified. Lack of repentance, or even insufficient repentance, allows for ever more neglect and falsification, so that we become more and more inconstant and therefore less likely to repent. The problem gets masked because we fear to become conscious of the gravity of the situation. We pretend simply because we fall into the way of it, not because we have calculated cause and effect of our action. And we pretend so hard because we fear the remorse, and the degree of it. Then, if we do feel remorse, we tend to leave it at that, as if something had been accomplished. But all that has happened is that for once a true human feeling has crept through our defences so that we have become conscious of the true state of affairs concerning our human being.

If we were to inquire directly into this state of affairs, we would discover first and foremost how difficult this is for us – because of our inconstancy. How can we even stand still long enough to find out what it means that we are human beings! Can we remain awake long enough to realize the extent to which we have inwardly fallen asleep? Does it matter to us that we are not at all what we are born to be? At least a single degree of constancy is required, one time, if we are to experience the remorse that must come with our having failed with a second degree of constancy, and then the repentance.

But what if a mask of self-pity is taken for repentance? What if the intention to be involved in an organic process of improvement is not forthcoming? Certainly we hope that in that case another will point us in the right direction. And we ourselves, if we know of the efficacy of repentance, may begin to build from that constant element at which we eventually arrive, in the knowledge that whatever is accomplished on that score, whatever people may say or not say, stands not for a time but for eternity.

Cults stand only for a time. Religions stand only for a time. The constant element can only be discovered by each one within himself. It is the pearl of great price. The way we impress one another with our familiarity with this element is formidable. If the illusion exists for us that we are human because we are born human, this can be made to serve.

(9/3/'96)

———————

23

Objective Science or Life-Goals

To trust appearance and not to suspect a delusion behind appearances, this is the chief of all life-goals. Not that appearances should be trusted. They disguise a mass of delusion. Certainly one has the choice, whether to suspect appearances or to trust appearance. In the former instance one searches for the truth, one refuses to be hoodwinked. In the latter case one is in possession of the truth an cannot be hoodwinked. One knows one cannot be hoodwinked. One feels free therefore to contribute to all that appears. In short one _is_ free to appear.

The freedom to appear is the greatest freedom of all. What we mean by life-goals here depends on this freedom. To move through space over a period of time in the awareness of space and time as home-grown fruits, so to speak, is truly a marvel, and this has to do primarily with all that occurs to us as we do so. These occurrences, these happenings, are experienced as miraculous. The names we give to them do not draw them out of context but leave them connected.

The search for truth, by comparison, while we mistrust appearances – or rather, once we have begun to mistrust appearances and while we find ourselves doing so – this search is always in a sense metaphysical, because we cannot believe what we see, nor what we feel, and this is experienced as a scandal. We are, as it were, scandalized by appearances. Appearance as such is only a dim possibility on our horizon. We get a glimpse now and again of what it might be like some day if we look at the face of reality and see reality, and this leads us on and lures us towards the truth. Meanwhile we think of the truth as somehow 'behind', or independent from, those appearances which time and again have shown themselves as unable to support an experience of reality. We cannot, for the time being and where we are, make out such a thing as appearance, and as true appearance, but only a multitude of appearances, which must all be dismissed as potentially or in fact false. We turn away from them and towards our heart or mind. Feeling and thought preoccupy us. Then these fall to pieces too, as feelings and thoughts, and once again we are betrayed. While we stand back, remaining uninvolved and uncommitted, appearances pileup for us wherever we look and listen and touch.

So we aim for objective science and for an objective reality. This means something very specific to us. Our ambition is now once and for all to knock these appearances into shape so that we can at least control them. Objectivity, not truth has become our goal. Then we equate truth with objectivity. Of course subjectivity might do just as well, but we have to start somewhere. The objective scientist in us has his work cut out for himself. He may collect myths or mushrooms, he may analyze souls or seismic shocks, his ambition is one and the same: to arrive at

143

an unalterable configuration of appearances on which he can pin his future hopes – his hopes for a future.

If instead we decide to trust appearance, we have the truth in us. We ourselves appear and join all that appears. We have nothing to do with appearances now, but we know that the truth appears, and that whatever appears must be true. If someone or something in our vicinity appears to be false, we right away appear on behalf of the thing or the one who appears like that.

We find out a little more meaningfully here what it means to appear, when we speak of appearing on behalf of someone or on behalf of something. The implication is, of course, that we have the choice of whether to appear or not. We can leave our mind to go through its various habitual routines while or body makes the customary moves, even while our soul itself becomes inactive. In the meantime we ourselves are, as it were, in hiding. Someone addresses us and discovers that no one is at home. I try to make not too much of a difference between appearance and existence here. Naturally we cannot appear if we do not exist. The important point seems to be that all our available faculties are put, by us, at the disposal of the one we know as the light of day. Initially we probably have a difficulty with this notion of the light of day as personal. We distinguish between the light of day and daylight. The one we know as the light of day makes it possible for us to appear.

*

It must seem entirely out of character for anyone with a capacity for recognizing life-goals to concentrate on objective (or subjective) understanding. We cannot really regard the objectivity as a necessary stage prior to the need to appear. It happens that children who 'need to appear' are incredibly frustrated by an educational emphasis on objective understanding and science. It must surely be recognized by educators today that a different kind of human being has entered the world, which will not be forced to mistrust appearances. The uninformed teacher

144

supposes that the child trusts appearances and feels obliged to guide him towards 'greater objectivity', when all the while the child does not trust appearances at all, but appearance. It is the teacher who has regard to appearances, and he must take care not to draw the pupil into his, the teacher's, unfortunate condition. In all fairness it must be admitted that the teacher comes ever closer to the truth without ever making real contact, while the pupil has the truth within him and knows it, so why should he not appear and equally place his complete trust in appearance?

If we have the truth in ourselves we need to show it. The need to show the truth, to manifest it, can become like an illness if it is not satisfied. So we must ask ourselves in all seriousness how this satisfaction may be gained. Evidently it makes no sense to search behind the phenomena of life. We do not even experience such things as phenomena. For the objective scientist there are many phenomena, and all of them desire to be the only one. He feels he must find ways of overcoming the egotism of individual phenomena. Sometimes the only way he can do this is by selecting some mystic entity and endowing it with an arbitrary sovereign quality, against which no phenomenon can succeed. We will not spend time here analyzing the objective scientist's problem, and we will not ask what would happen if he began by overcoming his own egotism. Instead we will recognize our own need, and the need of many today, to show the truth that is within them.

We do not search behind any phenomena but we lovingly accept all phenomena, refusing to judge. This loving, unjudgmental acceptance of all phenomena, of the phenomenal world as a whole, must become characteristic of the way we are and behave. We do not reject some phenomena in favour of others. The cosmos, the world – the universe, these are endless for us, and we feel perfectly at home with their being endless – with their endless being. Of course it occurs to us that our task is to show the truth, and so we set about giving some evidence of this endless phenomenality. Our knowledge is, that however we go, we cannot go wrong. Our understanding in turn touches on all those unexplored regions of reality of which those next to us so often seem to be afraid. So each one of us works out his or her own way of demonstrating to all who care to know and to understand how marvellously equipped we are, as human beings, to fit into the world, the cosmos and the universe. We show this by dealing confidently with whatever comes along which would seem to prevent us from doing that. More simply put, in the face of adversity we let the truth in ourselves speak for itself.

If at first it seems to us that the truth in ourselves speaks a language we cannot quite understand yet, we do not let that bother us. No one can be greater than the truth. It may happen that we speak today what we do not quite understand until tomorrow.

Or should we perhaps say that the truth which speaks in us, especially in the face of adversity, brings along with it its own power of perception, and sometimes we are slow to come around to that? There is an understanding of the head, of the heart, and of the hand. All three would pertain to the truth. Only as we combine all three do we gain the full satisfaction of genuine phenomenality as life. Only then is our goal achieved. No longer do we stray into the realm of abstraction out of fear of inertia, since that fear is overcome by trust. No longer do we arbitrate between opposing forces in ourselves and in the world but we let those forces take care of themselves while we concentrate on the live appearance of the truth. The fact that it appears wherever we look fills us with joy. The fact that its appearance is live amounts sometimes to something like an experience of terror, but then we live up to it.

Just as we may live up to the truth that appears live in our environment, so may we raise up our experience to the level of the truth that speaks live within us. To the objective scientist it must sound absurd, to raise one's experience to the level of the truth. He does after all presuppose a reality *out* there, separate from himself, just as the subjective scientist presupposes one *in* there, again separate from himself. Such a presupposition cannot possibly let the live truth appear, since it takes no account of humanity as the essence of being. It ignores the truth that resides in human relationship. But then, of course, it views human relationship in a much different light.

The way we extricate ourselves from objective and subjective realism has to do with the life goals we set ourselves. We may, for example, desire to cut through the fog of incomprehension that besets us in the face of misadventure. Armed with nothing but our desire for clarity we may wish to put paid once and for all to the lingering suspicion in our breast concerning the viability of a perfect existence in the light of day, here and now. We may no longer care for the rewards of cynical indifference to a static normality and insist instead on a compassionate response to what we see with our own eyes and hear with our own ears, quite irrespective of our fears of being hoodwinked and cheated.

Instead of life-goals we might do better to say live goals. But the main point is that in all our endeavours we remain within range of the powerful creative influence that would shape and change us. That our goals should ever more thoroughly coincide with the nature of this live influence, this must be our daily ambition and satisfaction.

For something to be live, such as an issue, a concern or an interest, it must enlist our intelligence, our feeling and our activity. It lies in our power to ensure that this is so. If only one of these three is left out, we have reverted to that extent to an alien way of life. To that degree then we have shut ourselves off from nourishment and we have nothing to give, so that decrepitude and degeneration set in.

So it is not enough that we tinker with our own individuality or the individuality of others. It won't do to presuppose a separate reality and then to study that from a distance. The goals we set ourselves must be such that they could just as readily have set themselves for us, and we shall not rest until we are fully encompassed by our goal and virtually one with it.

(13/3/'96)

24

The Nourishing Element

The fourth element we would like to discuss is the element of nourishment.

The time comes when nothing will do but we need to apply to our organic origin. Why is this often so much easier said than done? We seem to know more about what nourishes animals and plants than about the sustenance of human beings.

And yet there is something that can be assumed to be lying there ready for our immediate consumption. Or rather, it does not lie there, but it always arrives. It is the 'coming bread'. Our attitude here is of crucial importance. It is not a question of searching and finding or of reaching out and attaining. We go wrong if we make any effort towards the thing we want. And of course it is not a thing. Compare it to water that surrounds a fish and presses in on him. The fish is never aware of that pressure.

For the sake of discussion we can break it down into assumption and consumption. We begin by assuming that this element of nourishment exists and this is like opening our mouths. Remember that it does not appear, so we do not run the risk of mistaking for it something that appears, such as a pressure, a light, or a sensation of any type or kind.

We assume that it exists, as that which is given to sustain us. We may then find that a new sensation offers itself but we continue to assume instead of sensing. The 'instead' is important. If we opt for the sensation, or rather if we continue with it, we no longer eat. We no longer consume. So it depends on what we want. What begins as assumption continues as consumption as we return to assumption instead of sensation. We have described here an act of spiritual swallowing. No use trying to anticipate the sensation because a., we cannot know where it comes from and b., it has to happen. The sensation is really our accidental response, our reaction, to a morsel of sustenance, so we can take this sensation as evidence that sustenance is given. But we have not accepted it until we return to the nourishing element. Then that morsel is part of us.

At first the reaction will carry us away. We find ourselves day-dreaming, thinking about something or enjoying various sensations. Nothing in itself wrong with that, but we have set out to nourish ourselves. Did we not begin with all this because of hunger?

This hunger is described differently by everyone. One has to identify the problem before going for the solution. If you are hungry for bread, can you identify that? Probably, although many nowadays are confused even here. Their hunger for bread masks their hunger for – spirit. Shall we call it that? Call it a hunger for spirit. Life seems empty. Dissatisfaction with any- and everything rules. No one can please us. We are irritable, contemptible, insufferable. It's as if someone had invited us to a banquet and we had arrived at the table – to be offered stones, wood and grass. Disappointment, frustration – these lie uppermost. But in our present case we might always agree to say we are disappointed and frustrated, finally and on the last consideration, not with all those things and people we mention and accuse, but with – life. Yes, finally it happens that just plain life is a bore and a betrayal and we long for death, for an end to all these miseries. What has life to offer?

We ask that question as though it meant something. Why should life have something to offer? Life is itself that which is offered. All our miseries and disgusts are in fact signs, sensations, testifying to the fact that life has been offered. Why do we linger with our reaction to the offer rather than returning to that which is offered? Perhaps in some cases we are just plain ignorant of the facts. We have not been informed, or we have not yet acted on the information. Or perhaps we have not yet made a good habit of such action.

Very well, so we have identified a hunger for spirit. But perhaps spirit is nothing more than a word for us yet. Surely what we want is not just any old spirit, but good spirit. We want spirit that will do us good. That may go without saying, but not without meaning. If we don't know what we want we cannot get it, or, getting it, we are confused by it and perhaps we lose it again, we forfeit it ignorantly.

The hunger for good spirit is upon us. We experience a veritable famine of life. We may have said that life has betrayed us, leaving us so dismayed, but now we know that this is terrible nonsense. We have betrayed ourselves. But forget that. Start afresh. Never mind what you did to deserve what you got. Concentrate now on getting what you want. Write out a new order slip. All that you experience as bitterness and resentment – simply acknowledge that and then turn to that element of nourishment. No such thing, you say? Well, naturally, not so far, for you, because you do not so far assume that it exists. Instead you always indulge your pain and your anxiety. You are willing to accredit those, and probably because you can sense them.

The experience of spiritual famine does not stop as soon as you turn to the element of nourishment, to 'the coming bread'. It may still continue for a long time on the periphery, always moving to the forefront again so that you can show that you mean business, and what your business is. It has nothing to do with accepting your despondency. Certainly it makes no sense to fight it, but what counts is that you set our eye on something else, metaphorically speaking. And that you do it again and again.

Surely you must know how to assume! Some say they cannot believe, for who knows what reason, as though they had been falsified in their very core. Can you not assume except what you can sense? But you can assume whatever you like, no one is preventing you. Pretending is different. To pretend means to activate in some measure. There is no tension in assuming. The essence of every assumption is that you behave as though things or circumstances were such as you all the same cannot experience. I assume the train has arrived and go to the station to welcome my friend. I have no sensible evidence of the train's arrival.

So much depends on establishing good habits. The first move is usually the trickiest. But there is also something called beginner's luck. Our body, as feeling, or our mind, as thought, registers a spiritual advance, which then eludes us as soon as we settle down with it. We speak of having been 'touched' by the spirit. For a time we felt much more alive. Next we ask, of course: How can we intentionally repeat the unintentional? A delusion would be the result. Does that mean it must have been a delusion the first time? It was an illusion. We can learn from our illusions. It's when we try to repeat them that we go wrong.

Assume that spiritual nourishment insensibly presses in on you. Work on this assumption. It seems so contrary to all you have learned in the school of experience, and yet experience is nothing without it.

Of course we might say that the thing which most typically stands in the way of such an assumption is our own accumulated lot of sensuality. If we have aimed for complete satisfaction – no, if we have aimed for satisfaction – exclusively within the realm of experience where our senses might enjoy an eternal fulfilment, then we need to overcome a prejudice or two, namely against spirit. However if we have sought perfection solely in spirit, then this so-called pure spirit is bound in the end to leave us in the lurch, miserably forsaken.

151

Our notion of spirit and the flesh is at fault. Until we see flesh and spirit as one in the light of day we have no eternal fulfilment. But flesh and spirit are one, for us. Into that we must needs immerse our knowledge. Not whether or not we understand this, but that we allow our understanding to be shaped by it, this is what moves us along towards the goal.

So the nourishing element is not any more spiritual than carnal. And yet if we had begun by calling it carnal, would we not have been dreadfully misunderstood?

Try it. Call it carnal for a moment. Look out on the city with its gleaming roofs in the rain. Now take care, or thoughts will get in the way. Assume this element of nourishment – let this be the sum total of your thinking – as you face creatures and creation. You see, there is no such thing as the mere flesh, except for you if once you have contemptuously stepped back from the flesh – perhaps misguidedly in search of pure spirit. Forever we seem to try to correct one another's mistakes instead of simply doing it right. So the pendulum swings back and forth and we are historically fascinated, as time passes us by on the way to the eternal.

Not spirit, but good spirit has become flesh. That qualification must explain a lot. We need to limit ourselves to the good spirit before we can partake of this universal fulfilment, this cosmic perfection, this world without end; before we can understand ourselves as of necessity bound up with it. Every true perception of flesh and spirit as one presupposes a perception of myself by myself, of yourself by yourself, as privileged within the perspective and domain of good spirit. While we still flirt with irresponsible endlessness, or while we still indulge ourselves in a pious unwillingness, flesh and spirit in ourselves part, and then our cowardice and our cupidity manufacture evidence for self-justification. First we need to learn about reality from those who know it. Then we can bring ourselves around to that. The prize is humanity and life – not necessarily recognizable upon achievement to all and sundry, but without doubt to him who attains to them.

Knowledge of this allows us to proceed from consumption to consummation, because now suddenly, unexpectedly, we have what it takes to acquire, to ingest and imbibe, this nourishment – for others. The communal element plays into it. We are literally able to communicate eternal life. Reality reveals itself to us as whole, not just to me as whole, and consequently I am revealed to myself as whole because you too are revealed to yourself as whole. It sounds like an exercise in higher mathematics, but even at this moment I experience what I mean here and you have the benefit of it.

Human beings should not search for their real nourishment but they simply accept it. While they search for it, their minds and bodies manufacture thoughts and passions which effectively block out the food. In human beings the search for food is itself a blind reaction to the omnipresence and to the immediacy of food. When we find ourselves searching for food we should immediately cease and repair our vision and thought by turning instead to this element of nourishment, which may be initially assumed. The separate mentioning of assumption, consumption and consummation is to aid our understanding and skill. Once we are schooled and begin to practice, there is one single act and continuous action.

But we need to make heroic efforts initially, and not everyone who begins will complete the course. The struggle to survive is commonly preferred over the will to live, and massive machinery exists to keep things from changing. There is no hope for nations, for tribes, for dynasties; only for individual human beings, who live their lives for others and who work towards the establishment of human being.

An undernourished human being makes the mistake of substituting the thrill of creativity for life and thus loses both. The nourishing element is neither far away nor near, neither to be pursued nor awaited. It cannot be grasped and it cannot be re-sisted. Simply by not knowing that it exists and by not opening our mouths we forfeit our nourishment. Puny we become, and downright contemptible, for the lack of the invisible sustenance that is endlessly available to all who take upon themselves the common lot of humanity, an easy burden if carried with a will and never laid down.

—————

(23/3/96)

—————

www.ingramcontent.com/pod-product-compliance
Lightning Source LLC
Chambersburg PA
CBHW060515290526
45791CB00001B/391